BORN IN AFRICA

CHARLES ONYEGBULE UZOARU

authorHOUSE®

AuthorHouse™
1663 Liberty Drive
Bloomington, IN 47403
www.authorhouse.com
Phone: 1-800-839-8640

First published by AuthorHouse   09/15/2011

ISBN: 978-1-4567-9455-2 (sc)
ISBN: 978-1-4567-9454-5 (hc)
ISBN: 978-1-4567-9456-9 (ebk)

Library of Congress Control Number: 2011915689

Printed in the United States of America

DEDICATION:

To all African immigrants who left their homeland in search of a better life.

And, to those Africans who sacrifice their resources, time, talent, intellect, and energy to make Africa a better place for all.

INTRODUCTION:

Majid was born in Africa; a place where the rich wallowed in stupendous wealth while the poor languished in endless privation. The day he was born, his father picked him up and raised him up to the sky in gratitude to The Almighty. *'Had fertility been something administered by our fellow humans, who would have given me the opportunity to have a son?'* his father tearfully asked.

There were three predominant classes of people; the super-rich (a small percentage of the population), the super-poor (the overwhelming majority of the people), and the barely visible middle class sandwiched in between.

In a land blessed with immense human and natural resources, Majid belonged to the teeming majority of people that drowned in poverty and deprivation on a daily basis.

His parents fought poverty in a losing battle and died from it. As a result, he was left orphaned, disillusioned, helpless, and practically abandoned to his own fate. He decided to fight back and had one objective in mind: to reach and adopt the Promised Land.

America, he was told, was a land where streets were paved with gold and money grew on trees. Getting to America was his best means of avenging his parents' death. From there, he would battle, humiliate, destroy and bury poverty; the same thing poverty did to his parents.

It didn't matter to him if he ended up maimed, jailed, disabled or killed in the process of getting to the land of milk and honey. What else was he living for?

In practical terms, he was *already* dead. Because he still had intact cardio-pulmonary, neurological, physical, and intellectual functions, people failed to see the *dead* in him.

His life started in Africa from the gutter and he was determined to end it in America; on a high note. He was a very passionate young man; firm, determined, innovative and audacious.

Would his wish be fulfilled? Where and how might his life come to an end?

Only the future had the answers.

BORN IN AFRICA
(PART ONE: THE BEGINNING)

It is said that *'whatever has a beginning must have an end'*. Will this beginning have a desirable end? Time will tell.

Chapter 1.

At the naming ceremony, he was named Majid after his father. His birth was heralded by a sudden and unexpected downpour that was unusually heavy but short-lived. The sudden end of the unusual downpour coincided with the birth of Majid in the wee hours of the morning.

Almost as soon as he was born, the cock crowed and the domestic dog added his voice with few threatening barks in quick succession. There was a heightened sense of an impending period of hardship in the horizon.

The boy's father was a tall and burly man with an imposing figure. When he walked, the vibrations set off by his pounding footsteps could be felt from quite a distance. All his life, he worked hard to make ends meet. Yet, he lived and died a poor man.

Among his age mates, he was the last to take a wife. That was because; he didn't have the money to get married. At a point, he was given an *ultimatum* by the members of his age grade to either get married or be kicked out of the group. That was because he remained the only member of the group without a wife and children. He was degraded, castigated, taunted, insulted, and called derogatory names. When the pressure became unbearable, he got married with money that was borrowed from a neighbor.

His wife quickly got pregnant. Unfortunately, they were too poor to live a normal life and his wife could not seek proper medical or obstetrical care. As a result, her fate was left in the hands of Divine Providence. She was very sickly and no one thought she would survive the nine months of gestation. Amazingly, she did; and his son was delivered at home without professional help. That was how little Majid came into the world.

During his birth, Majid swallowed amniotic fluid and almost died. His survival was nothing short of a miracle. He came out of the womb blue and gasping for air with an occasional forceful gurgling sound. The village woman who assisted at the delivery quickly held the baby upside-down by the legs and slapped him a couple of times on the back. By the time the baby was quickly turned around with his head up, his color had improved and he started crying like a normal new-born baby.

As soon as the child was brought out from the make-shift delivery enclosure, his father quickly picked him up and raised him up to the sky in gratitude to the Almighty--

"Today, my seed has been officially sowed in the belly of humanity. Today, I claim reproductive equality with every man on earth, rich or poor, whose replicative ability has been established. Had fertility been something administered by our fellow humans, who would have given me the opportunity to have a son? Even if I die now, the embers left behind by my wretched life will continue to flicker and profess my existence among humans. Though I may die tomorrow, I'll leave behind a permanent imprint on the face of humanity"

Within weeks of his son's birth, the boy's father suffered a major social embarrassment. His creditor lost patience and called the police to arrest him for failing to pay back the money he had borrowed to marry his wife. He was sent straight to jail and his celebratory spirit was cut short.

His arrest and detention did not raise eyebrows. It was a common practice for anyone with money, power or the right connection to invite the police to arrest and jail someone; even for some trivial or fabricated offense.

While he was in jail, he suffered a cardiac arrest and died. As a result, he was deprived of that which every man passionately desired-- to tell his son moonlight stories, teach him hunting and farming, and groom him for adult life.

When Majid was barely six months old, his widowed mother

decided to give him up. The woman could no longer feed herself or the son she had brought into the world. She tried so hard to feed him breast milk. But, she couldn't. Her breasts had dried up and withered like dry meat. Besides, out of frustration or perhaps by instinct, the child had already stopped sucking the breasts.

In an effort to keep her dear son alive, the woman bundled him up and took him to the steps of a church building where, she hoped, someone might pick him up and give him a better life.

As soon as she put down the child, the little boy gave her a most wonderful smile; something that melted her heart. At that moment, she changed her mind and took him back.

Soon after that, Majid fell ill with high fever, jaundice and convulsions. A traditional healer, who was called to save his life, made a vertical incision on his mid-forehead and fed him some liquefied herbs to reverse the symptoms. Then, he applied a mixture of pigmentation, native dye and black paste of charcoal dust on the vertical incision to halt the bleeding. The wound healed quickly but left a pigmented mark on his mid-forehead.

Later, as he grew up, the facial mark earned Majid a nickname among his peers. They called him 'Cut-face'. Because of his sheer distaste for that nickname he practically hated himself and *avoided* looking at his face in a mirror.

The mere thought of a "mirror" would bring sadness to his heart and tears to his eyes.

One day, he braved a bathroom mirror and decided to look at his face. As soon as he confronted the mirror, something strange happened. Instead of seeing himself, he was confronted by what appeared to be his late father's image staring and *yelling* at him--

"Who said your face is ugly? Look at that scar very closely. It is a scar of life and good health; a scar that kept you alive.

There are scars of slavery used to classify the enslaved. You don't have them for you are a free son of the soil.

There are tribal scars used to identify one's origin. You don't have them for your root is not in question.

There are scars of humiliation used to mutilate the routed and those defeated in war. You don't have them for you have lost no battle.

There are scars of retribution used to distinguish captured thieves and evil men from others. You don't have them, for your hands are clean.

There are scars of attempted suicide sustained at the time of madness and desperation. You don't have them, for you are invincible in the face of adversity.

There are scars of revenge and jealousy used to disfigure those who are hated by others. You don't have them, for you are surrounded by love.

You are my son, and you must not look at your face with self-hatred.

When you hate your face, you end up hating yourself. And, when you hate yourself, you go from the visible, less harmful physical facial mark to a more destructive invisible mental scar.

The mental scar is the worst kind. It will inflame your system. It will suffocate you. It will cook you. It will boil you. It will roast you. And, it will fry you slowly into permanent desiccation".

At the end of that scolding tirade, the image vanished from the mirror. At that moment, Majid focused his attention on the scar; something he had never done before. He was no longer seeing his face but a scar that had suddenly assumed new and improved prominence.

He began to notice a few details about the scar. It was not crooked but straight. It was not rough but smooth. And, it was artistically crafted and centrally placed at the mid-forehead; equidistant from the lateral sides of the face. Rich in texture, it had a unique color that blended perfectly with the skin and made it look like an elegant artwork on a human canvas. That scar suddenly portrayed a unique picture of royalty; of dignity, beauty, and elegance.

His mind was filled with a spontaneous sense of pride and admiration--

"Who but an artist can beautify a human face in this manner with a small incision made in a hurry to save life?

This is amazing!

Who but a genius can pacify multiple furious convulsions with a simple cut made on the forehead?

This is wonderful!

Who but a gifted mind can effectively, yet harmlessly, halt an active bleeding with dust and native dye?

This is stunning!

A scar can be ugly; or beautiful. It depends on the location.

A mark can be hideous; or appealing. It depends on the details.

This scar is neither hideous nor repulsive. It gives credence to the intellect, the nobility, the brilliance of a noble ancestry.

It's only the ignorant mind that will find fault with a scar such as mine.

My eyes have been opened. I am truly my father's son"

From that day, Majid was no longer held hostage by a simple facial scar.

He had been *liberated!* He had advanced from his low level of destructive self-esteem to the height of an exhilarating self-confidence. He had come to know, appreciate and relate to the father he never knew in real life. He was his father's son; in flesh, blood and spirit. A simple facial scar had been transformed from an object of hate and misery to a symbol of dignity-- an avenue for reunion between a lost and invisible father and a revitalized, living son.

Majid grew up chasing rats and rabbits for food and running errands for a fee.

CHAPTER 2.

In those days, school headmasters were very much revered, feared and respected for their intelligence, social status, sense of discipline, and financial independence. They reminded everybody of the saying that *'when the lion enters the forest, the antelope scampers for safety'.* They were like lions in the midst of lesser animals and when they spoke, people listened. They bridged a gap between the old and the new; and between the local populace and the evolving white, foreign supremacy. They could 'interpret' the white man's language and culture. As a result, the white masters placed them in positions of authority to run the local schools, establish the white man's religion, and assist in enforcing their new laws.

Decoding the white man's language into local tongue was by no means an easy job. A school headmaster's interpretation of the white man's language could be so hilariously inaccurate. But then, there were few individuals with a fairly good command of both languages around to recognize the gross mistake.

The local school headmaster in Majid's district had a wife whose cruelty and disrespect for the lower class was unrivaled. Their children grew up callous, disrespectful and obnoxious like their mother. Everybody kept away from that family except those who were obligated or compelled to do otherwise.

In those days, jobs were very hard to find, especially for the lower class. Yet, each time the school headmaster sought a new maid or houseboy, only the most desperate job-seekers would bother to apply for the job. Even the needy were smart enough to shun the man's house, the same way they would avoid a plague.

Majid had just graduated from high school when the school headmaster announced that he was looking for a new houseboy. Majid applied for the job and was quickly accepted. He was ready and willing to do *any* type of job to support his poor mother and save some money for his college education. Serving as the school headmaster's houseboy turned out to be so traumatizing, so dehumanizing and so thorny for him. Yet, he loved it for the money. If Majid hated his job, he did not show it. He moved around with a straight face that revealed neither sentiments nor emotions. Perhaps, he was mindful of the proverb that says: *'that which a dog sees and barks, the sheep sees it and keeps quiet'.*

Once in a while, he would console himself--

"This is an awful job but it gives me hope.

This is a demeaning job but it gives me a chance to survive and take care of my mother".

There was a recent wave of kidnapping in the country which kept the well-to-do on the edge. Anyone with money or the means to quickly raise funds had suddenly become a target and no one, except the super protected, was exempt. Those living in areas that were distant from the centrally-localized security operatives were particularly vulnerable to abduction. Occasionally, folks in the villages, fearful for their lives and well-being would resort to sleeping in a nearby bush or forest at night. In order to maximize their profit, the kidnappers went a step further and devised *indirect* means of getting to those rich and well-protected individuals who were beyond their physical reach. They would kidnap their close or even distant relatives and family members and hold them hostage until ransom was paid. The government, unfortunately, seemed too powerless and impotent to stem the rising tide of insecurity in the land and protect the ordinary citizen.

That was the prevailing atmosphere in the land when Majid got his job as a houseboy. He was getting used to his new job when the school headmaster got kidnapped and was forced to pay a huge sum of money for his release. Like most teachers in those days, he wasn't a particularly rich man. So, most of the ransom money was *borrowed.* Upon his release from custody, the school headmaster was forced to terminate Majid's job because he could no longer afford the services of a houseboy.

The young mans spirit was down but not for too long. When a distant uncle heard of Majid's predicament, he showed up and volunteered to take the young man with him to the city.

"My family and I will love to have you with us in the city. I'm not rich enough to pay you salary. However, we can house you, feed you and take care of your basic needs. From the house, you can join other young people in the streets and hawk your way to survival," the uncle promised him.

The offer was like a dream come true. Majid thanked the man profusely and promised to be a good house boy as well.

His mother couldn't be happier.

"When you get there, my son, please don't bring back shame to our home. There is a saying that 'when they laugh at your bag, it's you they are laughing at'. Any shame on you is shame on this family. Respect and obey your uncle and his wife at all times. Keep their house clean and take good care of their children. It is said that 'the same god that gave yams to a child will give him the sharpened stick to dig them out'. God gave you life and will provide you with the means to stay alive. 'A cow without a tail has its deity to chase away the flies'. We may not have anybody on our side. Yet, God is there for us at all times," she advised her son.

To get to the city, Majid needed a bus ticket. It would be his first time to ride in a bus. He went to the bus station where he queued in line for a ticket like a disciplined soldier trained to obey simple rules.

The line was long. Initially, everything was very smooth, orderly and peaceful.

Then, the line in front of him started to branch into two. As more people tried to get in front of everybody else, the line grew tentacles, became shortened and quickly distended into a dynamic mass of energized bodies. From pushing to shoving to near physical fight, people resorted to various types of aggressive behavior as each person tried to get in front of others. Everybody was talking and yelling at the same time.

The room suddenly became warm and stuffy as people breathed and puffed repeatedly in a rising fashion. The air quickly turned humid and musty--a combination of floating dusts and stale odor of human perspiration. Majid was not used to the prevailing physical chaos. Unfortunately, he had to get to the city like everybody else; so he joined the madness. Someone almost tore the shirt off his sweaty body; a testimonial to his lack of experience at crowd fight.

As if the rising chaos was not irritating enough, an angry little man who was panting like an oxygen-deprived animal broke loose from the crowd and flared up in the face of a fat ugly fellow.

"If you dare to push me again, I will kill you," he yelled.

"You better watch what you say! It's said that 'when the mouth leads the war, the foot does not return'. You must be insane to threaten someone ten times your size and strength. 'What can a mouse achieve from biting the foot of a cow?'"

"Are you calling me a mouse you fat ugly coward? It's said that 'the bee is a small neighbor. But, nobody pockets it, or covers it with a fist,' the little man yelled back.

The fat fellow simply bumped his belly into the lean man and sent him crashing backwards.

"Now, let's see who is a coward among us," he taunted the small man.

Meanwhile, the girl at the ticket counter feigned ignorance of the madness unfolding before her. It is said that *'a dangerous dog is not the one that barks the most, but the one that bites the most'.* With her pretty facial outlook, silent demeanor and feminine composure, one could quickly mistake her for 'a walkover'. In reality, she knew how to discipline an unruly crowd. Pretending to be busy doing nothing, she took her time to pull a couple of drawers in and out; in and out. At the same time, she totally ignored the unruly customers fighting each other for her attention.

Suddenly, she stood up from behind the counter and disappeared into a dark corridor leading to the employee bathroom. She had learnt from experience that the best way to pacify an unruly crowd was to set a price for any disruptive behavior. She went to the bathroom mirror where she looked at her image and gave vent to her pent-up emotions--

"It is said that 'a dancer dances to the rhythm of the music'. If these folks want me to serve them, they have to behave appropriately. 'An itch is not the same thing as a tickle'. They think I'm tickled by their itching behavior.

What exactly are they fighting for? They pant and yell and gasp and shove one another; they suffocate everybody with dust and the stale odor of human perspiration. Sometimes I feel like a punching bag designed for the agitated world to vent their frustrations on".

By the time she got back to the ticket counter half an hour later, there was calm and order. The crowd had gotten the message.

Two hours later, everyone had purchased a bus ticket. The entire process could have taken just thirty minutes if it had been carried out in an orderly fashion.

Finally, it was time to board the bus that was already three hours late. The passengers were already gearing up for the next imminent fight. Every passenger wanted to be the *first* person to enter the bus.

At the end of the protracted drama, all the passengers were finally seated for the long ride to the city.

Majid couldn't help wondering what the pushing and shoving and yelling were all about--

"Those who call us 'the happiest people on earth' must be right.

In this country, there are two notable classes of people. The first, upper and superior class belongs to the rich and powerful while we, the downtrodden, are the members of the second, lower and inferior class.

The two classes seem to be bonded in a symbiotic yet baffling form of relationship.

The upper class is made up of sadists who derive extreme pleasure in torturing, punishing, and humiliating the rest of us. They beat us, they flog us, they jail us, they starve us, and they deny us the most basic forms of human dignity and freedom. They flaunt and squander our collective wealth while we cheer them on and reward them with titles, accolades, and numerous awards. In spite of their multiple atrocities, they'll do anything to maintain their "good name" and will not hesitate to burn down entire buildings, cause confusion, uproot institutions, destroy documents and eliminate lives in order to cover their tracks.

The lower class is made up of masochists; the rest of us. First, we submit to the will of the sadists, and we make them happy. Then, we turn around and make our own lives unlivable. For every simple task, we act like the two proverbial foolish goats trying to cross a very narrow bridge both at the same time. We shove, we sweat, we curse, and we pant and gasp for air. Our blood pressure rises. We pollute the air with nasty body sweat and odor. At the end, we are physically exhausted and emotionally drained and we look like fools coming out of a dungeon. One begins to wonder if the adrenaline rush clouds our sense of judgment with the exhilaration that comes with it.

Both sadists and masochists must indeed be meant for each other.

Each time we create problems for ourselves where none exists, the sadists watch from a distance with utter glee.

While the sadists bully their way through with stolen wealth and common resources, the masochists seize every opportunity to applaud and crown them with accolades and lofty titles.

One class claims ownership of dignity, respect and freedom while the other is forced into a state of ignominy, abuse and captivity. We must, indeed, be so meant for each other that we have become 'the happiest people on earth'.

CHAPTER 3.

Majid got to the city and quickly settled down to business in his newly-found home. He practically took care of all the chores in the house and got along very well with the children. His hosts were as happy with him as he was with them.

During the day, he would take his petty goods and join other hawkers in the streets for a couple of hours. He managed his resources very prudently and took pains to re-invest every profit he made.

As time went on, his business grew. He went from cheap petty goods to quality products that brought him more gains.

One day, he was in the midst of his fellow hawkers when, suddenly, a siren was heard blaring towards their direction. Everybody scampered for safety. Some of the hawkers even *abandoned* their wares as they ran away from the scene.

Majid could not understand what the commotion was all about. He had never witnessed anything like that in his life. He remembered the proverb that says: *'if you see your age mates running, join them for you alone cannot stop whatever is chasing them'* He tried to gather his things quickly and run like others.

Unfortunately, he was not as fast as his fellow hawkers.

A police jeep filled with stern-looking, whip-flashing constables caught up with him. One of officers stretched out his hand and lashed him several times with a horsewhip. His flesh was practically ripped off by the vicious attack. Seconds after he had fled from the scene in severe pain, a siren-blaring motorcade accompanying the governor of the State passed through at top speed.

That was when he realized why people were running so abruptly for their lives.

The governor was passing through the area and anyone who dared to block the road could be whipped, beaten or even jailed without charge. *'When a pebble rises, the clay pot begins to tremble'.* The high and mighty had become the proverbial "pebble" against the common man.

Majid was reminded of the saying that *'one who is hated does not stoop by the wayside'.* The common man must be so *hated* by the mighty that he could no longer find peace standing by the wayside.

"Why do the mighty hate us so much?" he wondered.

The life he witnessed regularly in the city amplified the big gap between the rich and the poor. All year round, the downtrodden never had it easy. Life was a constant struggle.

During the rainy season, they endured constant abuses and humiliation from Mother Nature and humans alike. Surrounded by expanding ravines and gullies that encroached upon their habitat, they lived in homes that dripped rainwater and emitted the stale odor of molds and humid decay. On the public roads, cars would drive into ditches and pockets of flood water and splatter them with dirt and human waste.

The dry season did not spare them either. It brought along suffocating heat and humidity coupled with showers and stains of brown dust. One minute, their clothes would be soaked by human perspiration. Next minute, the same clothes would be dried off by their body heat.

Life on the streets was harsh and brutal for the hawkers. It was a world where the fittest reigned supreme. Pervasive criminality, banditry, fist-fights and pick-pocketing were the determinants of supremacy and leadership in the street world.

Sometimes, the police would descend on them with one objective in mind; to fabricate lies and *extract bribes* from the struggling hawkers for crimes they never committed.

It was during one of those *illegal* raids that Majid was picked up, beaten and sent to jail. While he was there, his host and distant uncle, refused to get involved. He had neither the money nor the right connection to do anything on Majid's behalf. During his days in jail, Majid became a feast for bed-buds, crabs and hungry mosquitoes.

On the first day, he slept on the cold bare floor. Then, he became ill with high fever on the second day. That was when they let him sleep on a bug-infested bed with tattered mattress. He had not eaten in two days. His skin and sclera were jaundiced and his urine turned yellow. Someone thought he had acute malaria. But, a long-term inmate had a different idea. He could swear that Majid had hepatitis infection or liver disease. He had seen too many of such cases.

When it dawned on the prison authorities that Majid had no one to 'bail' him out and that he might *die* in prison, they released him.

Not long after his jail-term, Majid was hawking edible items--bananas, oranges and roasted peanuts--when a white man came to a stop in a traffic jam. From all angles, the hawkers *swarmed* on the white man like excited bees.

Majid followed suit, hoping to make a handsome sell.

The white man was sitting inside his car with a well-groomed, hefty dog. When Majid saw the white-man's dog, he shook his head with amazement.

"You seem to like dogs, don't you?" the white man asked him while ignoring the army of hawkers surrounding him.

Obviously, the white man was not particularly interested in *buying* anything.

"Frankly speaking, sir, I hate dogs. But this is no ordinary dog. This is more like a king in his own domain," Majid responded with awe.

"Would you then like to walk him and give him bath for a fee?" the white man asked?

"Sir, who in my shoes, will refuse to walk and bathe a king for a fee? It's like getting a promotion from being a hawker to becoming a royal servant," he replied with childlike giggles.

"What makes you call this particular dog a king?"

"Sir, this dog has class. It has dignity and exceptional freedom. It has an air of superiority, might and power"

"Seriously speaking, you can walk him and bathe him every morning for a handsome fee. That won't interfere with your daily hawking activities"

"Sir, you sound serious, don't you?" Majid asked with a serious face.

"I couldn't be more serious in my life. I seem to like you. That's why I'm offering you the job"

"For a handsome fee; why not? When do I start my new job, sir?"

"You can start work tomorrow morning at 8 o'clock. I live a few blocks down the road. Here is my home address," the white man replied, handing Majid a business card.

"Thank you sir; I will be there"

Majid was granted permission by his hosts to accept the job. That was the beginning of a relationship that seemed to spring out of nowhere. He took his new job seriously, and tried to make the best of it. With time, he began to *develop* mixed feelings of likeness, curiosity, envy, pity and disdain for the white man's dog.

One day, Majid confronted the dog in what appeared like a gazing *contest*. He gazed at the dog and the dog gazed back at him. Without realizing it, he was actually *transferring* his *scornful* feelings for the members of the upper class to a less defensible dog.

"What are you staring at me like that for?" Majid asked the dog.

Majid was *indirectly* talking to the *sadists* who, as it turned out, were completely beyond his reach. Confronting their dog, therefore, was as far as he could get to them.

The dog growled and Majid 'interpreted' it as a willingness to talk; so he continued.

"I bet you think and reason the same way as the leaders and rulers of this land; and why not? You are like one of them. You live, you eat, you sleep, and you bark like them. You bask in your exclusive world of leisure, abundance and waste. You dine and wine with reckless abandon. Any time you snap your doggy fingers,

your human servant responds with trepidation. Can I ask you something?"

The dog made a yapping sound which Majid, once again, *'interpreted'* as a positive nod.

"Have you ever come across your cousins in the village? Those dogs, unlike you, have to fight for every piece of rotten food that comes their way. They are constantly abused, starved, and discarded like inanimate objects. I know you will never appreciate their plight. But, I do. Sometimes, I feel like I'm one of them. Now, tell me; don't you feel guilty in your exclusive domain while your cousins are out there suffering?"

The dog snarled back at Majid in apparent 'anger'. Strangely enough, Majid's mind could 'interpret' every *'spoken word'* coming out of the dog's mouth in defense of the upper class--

"Don't be too hard on yourself. That's the problem with you, the downtrodden. Did you ever think you could get a great job that pays this good just for walking, feeding and bathing a dog like me? I didn't get to my upper level of hierarchy in one day. With patience and good luck, my cousins in the village will get to that level when their time comes. Besides, they are** not **complaining. It's ungrateful people like you who** poison **their minds and turn them against us".

"You know, I'm beginning to wish that me and you could exchange places; perhaps for one day. Then, you will know what it feels like to belong to the lower class. Look at you; you have everything that I don't have. You sleep and eat well; I don't. You have the type of luxurious home that I can only dream about. On top of that, you have me; a high school human graduate as a servant. Any time you lift a finger, it's to beckon a paid graduate servant to your side. When I lift a hand, it's to serve as a beast of burden. Someone walks you around, takes you bath, cleans your mess, feeds you on schedule, and takes you to the veterinarian for regular checkups. I can't even afford to go to the doctor; not to talk of someone taking me there. Oh, lest I forget; you're right. I should feel greatly honored that I'm serving you. It even makes me feel like I'm part of the upper class. I am truly grateful," Majid 'responded'.

In 'response', the dog made what sounded like a 'conciliatory' sound.

"Oh, don't be so silly! To start with, do you think it is *easy* **being on top? It is said that** *'when a rich man recounts what he went through to get rich, the poor man decides to remain where he is'.* **You don't know what I go through in life! I had always** *wished* **I could be** *human* **like you!** *Imagine! They call me* **a dog;** *that demeaning, derogatory name. Do you* **know what it** *feels* **like to be called a dog? They put me on a leach and they drag me around. That's the same way you treat your slaves, isn't it? They lock me inside the house all day, afraid that I might go astray. I have limited freedom. Is that the type of** *life* **you and my cousins in the village want? You must be a masochist indeed to want to be like me! It's said that** *'tomorrow is pregnant and no one knows what it will deliver'.* **You might even** *own* **a dog or many dogs like me tomorrow. Can I own you?"** the dog 'asked'

"Oh, you have the same guilt-inducing sarcastic tongue as our oppressors, the Sadists. They'll even tell you how good you have it and how hard they work for you. They'll tell you they have less freedom than you. In the same breadth, they'll ask you to stay where you are and 'get used to it'. Talking of freedom, your cousins in the village have 'freedom' indeed! They stray around all day fighting for human feces and left-over carcass. In the process, they are chased around and abused. Sometimes, they even get killed.

That's the type 'freedom' you're yearning for. I can see you're getting bored. Besides, it's time for your bath. Let me give you a bath before I lose my very prestigious job," Majid 'responded'.

Luckily for Majid, no one was around to see him 'arguing' with a dog. He was exhibiting the signs and behavior of someone who was traditionally labeled as 'insane', 'psychotic', 'delusional' or simply 'mad'. Such people were known to fight and argue with the rebellious inner self or with some invisible forces. It was not unusual for them to perceive canine creatures as human beings in hiding.

Soon after that 'argument' with a dog, Majid's mother fell ill in the village and was rushed to the local hospital. The same day he got the news of his mother's illness, Majid took the next bus home.

His employer, the white man was generous enough to give him all the money he might need for his mother's care.

"You have been a good boy; humble and loyal. There's a proverb that says, 'If a baby goat kneels down, it will be able to suck its mother's breasts'. You deserve a nice reward for your good behavior. I hope your mother gets well quickly," the white man said to him.

Unfortunately, by the time Majid got home, his mother was already *dead*. She died, *untreated,* on the hospital corridor. The doctors had *refused* to treat her because she was unable to make the initial deposit for her treatment. That was the standard practice at the time. Because poor patients would often walk away from the hospital with unpaid bills, the doctors adopted a stringent measure to withhold treatment until a deposit was made.

"It is said that 'you can't claim to be carrying someone on your back when the feet are dragging along the rough road'. How can people die, untreated, on the corridors of the same hospitals that claim to be saving people's lives?" Majid asked himself.

Before walking away from the grave, he made what sounded like a *farewell* speech to his mother:

It is said that *'when fire dies out, the ash remains to bear witness to the flames'. Mother, you are dead. But, your ash remains in me to bear witness to your glorious existence on earth".*

He left the grave filled with silent lamentations--

"Poverty, you have robed me of that which is most precious to me. You did so without regard to my feelings or humanity. It is time for me to fight back and get even. It's said that 'when someone bites your skull without regard to the brain, when you bite his or her behind, you'll do so without regard to the feces'.

Poverty, you have declared war between me and you. Now, it's either you kill me, or I bury you once and for all.

The sadists have turned this nation into a land of contradictions. On the one hand, we are blessed with abundant natural and human resources. Yet, we are bedeviled with intolerable woes of human adversity.

In a land where individuals fly overseas for simple medical check-up, our children and parents die, untreated, in glorified hospitals that are neither well equipped nor adequately staffed.

In a land where individuals own private jets and fleets of the worlds most expensive cars, our children and parents are sacrificed on pot-hole ridden highways as they ride like packed sardines in vehicles with unsound engines, worn-out tires and faulty brakes.

In a land where individuals send their children to the best schools abroad, our children and grandchildren are forced to waste their brains and talents in crowded, dilapidated and unhealthy school buildings with neither trained teachers nor equipment or adequate reading materials.

In a land where individuals can import entire hospital facilities for personal use, our children and parents are denied the cheapest medical technology and genuine medications for proper medical care. They are forced into the ungodly hands of quacks, voodoo priests and medical magicians.

In a land where individuals own some of the most expensive stone and marble houses around the world, our children and parents are forced to squat in tiny humid rooms and apartments with neither proper drainage nor adequate toilet facilities. There is no running water and no electricity.

When the poor dies, he's treated and buried like a worthless millipede with neither home nor ancestry. When the rich dies, the poor begins to hunger for death after witnessing the grandiose funeral ceremony.

In a land where individuals can afford constant protection from a platoon of soldiers and well-equipped policeman and women, our children and parents are left at the mercy of ravenous predators-- armed robbers, kidnappers, and ritualists. Sometimes, the victim is even forced to prepare a good meal for those who have come to perpetuate the evil acts.

In a land where individuals can feed an entire population, house them, clothe them, employ them, and educate them, our brothers and sisters die in foreign lands in pursuit of survival. They die in deserts; they drown in make-shift rafts and boats; they rot in foreign jails and they are turned into sex slaves and abused laborers in perpetual captivity"

After burying his mother like a man, he returned to the city.

That was when he made a firm decision to find his way into the white man's land.

His parents fought poverty in a losing battle and died from it. As a result, he was left orphaned, disillusioned, helpless, and practically abandoned to his own fate. He decided to fight back and had one objective in mind: to reach and adopt the Promised Land.

America, he was told, was a land where streets were paved with gold and money grew on trees. Getting to America was his best means of avenging his parents' death. From there, he would battle, humiliate, destroy and bury poverty; the same thing poverty did to his parents.

It didn't matter to him if he ended up maimed, jailed, disabled or killed in the process of reaching his destination. What else was he living for? He was passionate. He was determined. He was going to be innovative, audacious and unrelenting in his pursuit of justice. And, his decision was final.

He knew he might *die* in the process. That wouldn't matter; after all, he was already *dead;* practically speaking. He was simply the 'living' dead as opposed to the 'deceased' dead.

His mind told him so--

"Unlike the 'deceased' dead, I can still see, hear, speak, eat and drink like everyone else who is alive.

Unfortunately, while the 'deceased' dead are at peace; I am not.

Unlike me, they are invisible and beyond the reach of human misery.

I'm here to be kicked around, whipped and splattered with soiled water and human waste.

They don't have to worry about feeding, clothing, housing, and good health as I do.

I even have to bathe and walk a dog in order to survive.

In a white man's land I might, perhaps, find a higher-paying job taking care of dogs, fowls and goats. I could quickly learn to sleep with them and eat their left-over meals.

With some luck, I might even get a promotion to cater for human cadaver. Who would do a better job catering for the dead than someone who is already deceased?"

He couldn't help thinking of the numerous opportunities that would be available to him in the land of milk and honey.

Majid sold one of his two remaining parcels of land and decided to "purchase" a visitor's visa to America. He knew he would never want to come back to a country that had stripped him of all hope and human dignity. Yet, he left a parcel of land unsold-- just in case.

Everybody knew how difficult it was for a poor helpless immigrant to get to America. Many people had tried it; and failed. Some would get to America only to be jailed and bundled back to their country of origin.

There was a saying that *'the thought which led someone into suicide was not nurtured in one day'*. Obviously, Majid had spent a good quality time weighing the prospects of his potentially suicidal attempt to reach the American soil.

He was introduced to someone who would facilitate the visa process. Majid paid for the procurement of an international passport and an American visa.

The visa facilitator did not fail to spell out the risks involved in travelling to America with a 'purchased' and 'unofficial' visa--

"There is no guarantee that your mission will succeed. 'One does not test the depth of the river with both legs at the same time'. I will advice you not to bet all of your resources on this venture. A visa procured in this manner may or may not be genuine. As a result, you could be stopped at the airport and sent right back. You could be jailed for trying to enter the country illegally. Or, you could be lucky and slip through immigration. Even if the visa is genuine and you make it there successfully, you'll be on your own unless someone is willing to assist you. Legally, you can't work in America with a visitor's visa. So, you could end up on the street as a beggar trying to survive. If you get into trouble, it will be futile for you to implicate me in any way. I'm good at what I do and my tracks are professionally covered".

He was blunt and truthful.

"It is said that 'a rock at the bottom of the sea does not fear rain'. I'm already

dead here, so what difference does it make? I'm willing to take the chances. *'When the forest is on fire, the antelope ceases to fear the hunter's bullet'. What can be worse than the situation I'm presently in? But, frankly speaking, I don't expect the journey to be an easy one for me. 'A wise fish knows that a beautiful worm can have dangerous hooks,'"* Majid replied.

"*I will introduce you to someone who understands the travails of a vulnerable new immigrant in the America system; a friend from this country who 'died' several times before resurrecting into the American system. His bitter experience turned him into a Good Samaritan of some sort. He tries to help every genuine person who gets stranded in America. But, he can only harbor you on a temporary basis for as long as your visa is valid. Good luck in your endeavors".*

"*I'm truly grateful for your assistance," Majid replied with heart-felt gratitude*

He was in high spirits--

"*America, here I come! You can let me rot in jail. You can force me back home. You can let me die in your bosom. Or, you can give me a chance to battle poverty once and for all from your domain. The choice is yours,"*

He felt like someone who had already gained a foothold in America.

CHAPTER 4.

On the eve of his departure to the United States, his fellow hawkers threw an elaborate party for him in one of the open fields. They were happy that one of their own was going go to the white man's land. Someday, Majid could even become 'somebody' and make the rest of them proud. There was plenty of alcohol, food and joyful music to keep their spirits high till the wee hours of the night.

Then, they took turns to advise Majid on the best way to survive in America and avoid costly mistakes.

---*"Be careful with those American women. First, they will lure you into lurid sexual acts with their half-naked bodies; then they'll blind you with romantic perfumes. And once you fall into their trap, you'll be locked up in a human cage of deceitful marriage with little or no room to escape. It's said that 'when an animal falls into a trap, the proposed journey comes to an end'. If you're caged in by one of those women, your life's ambition will come to an abrupt end. 'A crab conquered great waters and seas only to drown in an old woman's soup pot'. Don't drown in an American woman's bosom after surviving years of endemic brutality of our tough terrain,"* one of the hawkers started.

Perhaps everyone was waiting for someone to speak first. As soon as the first speaker sat down, the 'words of advice' started flying in Majid's face from all angles.

---*"You must listen to us now with both ears. An adage says that 'when an insect falls deaf, it ends up in the belly of a noisy bird'. Whatever you do, don't bring a white woman home. Your parents will come out of their graves and slap you in broad daylight. When a white woman gets* tired of you, she'll kick you to the curb. In the words of the elders, 'a *twig that embraces a palm tree should know that they could never be siblings'*. You will become the proverbial twig embracing a palm tree if you marry a white woman. Stay away from them because they are not your type," the second speaker warned him.

---"Don't underestimate the intelligence of our people or their ability to gather information. *'No matter how high the bird flies, the ground will see its belly'*. If you commit any crime or stupid act in America, people here will get to know the details. As a proverb says, *'a fly without an adviser follows the corpse to the grave'*. If you don't listen to words of advice, you'll become that fly," said another.

---"You are going to the land of guns and drugs. It is said that *'only a tree hears that it's going to be cut down and it stands still'*. Don't' behave like a tree. Run away from places of excitement and commotion. Whenever you see those flashy cars blaring loud music and adorned by pretty girls, you must run for your life before drug dealers and cult members catch up with you. Watch out for stray bullets. They are everywhere!" another hawker lent his voice.

Majid listened, politely, without indicating what was going through his mind.

---"Don't live on the fast lane. *'The turtle says that speed kills'*. Some people push drugs to get rich quickly. Don't do it. There's a saying that *'When a child decides to run after an evil bat, he gets lost in the evil forest'*. Don't chase after quick wealth or else you'll end up in the dungeon. In the words of the elders, *'the same rain that spares the lizard soaks the rat severely'*. If you commit the same crime as an America, your punishment may be greater. *Besides, America is not this country where you can bribe yourself out of jail. Over there they'll lock you up and throw the keys into the Pacific Ocean. There's an adage that says, 'If I'm not like others, I don't mimic their ways'. Don't follow those who don't value their life, or the family they come from. Remember, 'Any ant dipped into a pot of oil can never come out unsoiled'. Every stupid act has its consequence*".

Majid simply sat there, passively, listening to numerous words of advice.

The next 'adviser' was a village comedian who always made people laugh by simply opening his mouth

---"When you get there, always remember that Americans don't *appreciate criticisms or blunt negative truths. Make sure you flatter everybody and everything that comes your way. Tell the ugly how so beautiful they are. If a woman's cooking tastes like garbage, tell her she cooks better than your mother; and beg her for the recipe. If you see someone wearing an outfit meant for clowns and monsters, sing words of praise and admiration. And remember; tell people you notice their perfect figure, even those who look like cows and pumpkins. Old age is a common enemy in America, so be sure to swear to a ninety-year-old woman that she looks sixteen. Sixteen is like the magic age when everything in life is so sweet. They call it 'sweet sixteen'. No matter how obnoxious or irritating a child may be, remain cool and tolerant and call that child 'cute', especially if a parent is around and watching. If you follow these social commandments, you'll enjoy the fruits of the American paradise"*

He kept everybody laughing.

---*"Be nice to their dogs! There's a proverb which says that 'a Tiger does not stand aloof while someone hurts the offspring'. Some of those Americans love their dogs more than they love their neighbor. Even if all you do is hurt the dog's feelings, your eyes might see your ears without a mirror,"* said another.

---*"America is a land of stress. A majority of the faces you see on the streets are distorted by pain, stress and misery. Sometimes you wonder why people look so miserable. Don't be deceived by the fake and plastic smiles on people's faces, especially in public gatherings and social events. Not all of it is real. Don't go greeting people you come across on the street and in public places like we do here. They'll think you are crazy".*

"How do you guys stay in this country and know everything going on in America?" Majid asked to everybody's hearing.

Nobody seemed to pay any attention to his question.

---*"Watch what you eat, brother, when you get there. Remember the saying: 'I'll rather go hungry than to black out from bulimia'. America is a land of fattening, junk food. You are going to see lots of people with bulging stomach hanging out like accessory organs. These are the same people who'll swear they are on diet and never eat a full meal! Always eat foo-foo, and clean your teeth with chewing stick. If you don't find real foo-foo, think of a substitute. Don't rely on* tooth-paste and tooth-brush alone. If you don't remove remnants of food particles and debris from your tooth cracks, you'll end up with germs, cavities and tooth abscesses. The white man's dentists are always smiling to the bank while the dentists in this country frown with empty pockets. Here, no one depends on a dentist to clean the teeth and remove food particles from the cracks. Why do you think the white man chews gums and sprays his mouth with breadth fresheners prior to a romantic date with his girlfriend?"

People laughed freely with each 'advice' given to Majid.

---"In a place like America, it is easy to forget who, and what you are. 'No matter how much the butterfly flies and flutters its wings, it can never become a bird'. Another proverb says that 'though the crocodile may live in water, it will never be a fish'. Don't try to be that which you are not. 'One does not learn to use the left hand in old age'. The moment you start changing your accents and bleaching your skin white, you'll begin to sound strange and lose your identity. It is common knowledge that America is a land of discrimination. No matter what, or who you are in that black skin of yours, people will see darkness rather than the real you. Even if you conquer the skies, they will remember your skin and not the achievement you made. In the words of the elders, 'when a hunter learns to shoot without missing, the bird learns to fly without perching'. Stay alert and focused at all times and don't fall victim to numerous tricky situations. Do the right thing, and come back safely to us. Personally, I'm not worried about you. 'We know our kinsman who will not disgrace us abroad by consuming every piece of food on the plate'. You will not disappoint us. A proverb says that 'if the ear goes to war against advice, it will fall off as well when the head is cut off'. I know you have listening ears and will come back to us intact. Have a safe, sound and pleasant trip my friend. And may the road protect you".

Thank you, my friend," Majid replied.

There was this young man among them who looked like a stick on two legs. The called him "Mosquito". He could eat and drink more than *all* the hawkers combined. Yet, he would *never* gain weight. His fellow hawkers always teased him about the 'worms' in his stomach that swallowed everything he ate. Some people nicknamed him *"Obesity is from above"*. When he stepped forward to give his own lengthy 'advice', people held their breath.

---"*Boy, I wish I were in your shoes! When you get to America, grab one of those white women, and don't let go. Marry one of them and settle down there. Look at this country where we live. What do you see? Devastation! Inordinate greed! Despair! Empty dreams! Broken promises! Pot holes! Insecurity! Abject poverty! Religious hypocrisy! Holy Ghost fire brigade! Professional gossipers! Widow chasers! Sugar daddies! Smoke screens! Epileptic utilities! Inflated contracts! Phantom payrolls! Political harlots! Misplaced priorities! Advance-fee fraud! Elephant projects! Treasury looters! Get married there, and settle down. Don't let anybody convince you otherwise. Going to America, my brother is like climbing the Iroko tree. It's something you can only achieve once in a lifetime! How many people are able to get there? In a desperate attempt to reach that land, some folks die on the road from starvation, suffocation and dehydration; or as victims of various crimes. 'He who gets to the top of the Iroko tree must collect all the firewood he can'. Get everything you can while you're there, including an American wife. Then, settle down there, have great fun and forget this wretched homeland. There's a saying that 'a blind man does not let go the snail his foot stumbles into'. You have stumbled into the America dream like a blind man. Don't let go! Here, take this photograph of mine. Show it to everybody you come across. Tell them I'm a homeless orphan and a beggar. You could come across some Good Samaritan who might be willing to assist me. When you get there, find me an American wife, even if she is lame, blind or crippled. I'll marry her; no questions asked*".

Everybody laughed.

The party went on all night. It was full moon, and one of those few days when festivity, relaxation and good humor would take the place of destitution and hardship in the midst of the hawkers.

Chapter 5.

Majid was told to be at the airport *three* hours prior to his departure time. He wanted to be there much earlier. Given a chance, he would even prefer to sleep at the airport.

Good a thing he flagged down a taxi *six* hours earlier to take him to the airport. It was raining hard and the roads were practically flooded. The taxi broke down on the road in a very obscure location. From where he was, it took him *one* hour to find another taxi going to the airport. When he finally waved down the second taxi, he pressured the driver to speed to the airport. It was a ride he would never forget in a hurry.

The doors of the taxi were held in place by welded bolts and his feet were soaked with flood water streaming steadily from underneath the car. Each time the taxi went through a pothole, he had a violent shock to the head that felt like a sudden migraine headache. The brakes were squeaking, the tires were ready to disintegrate at any moment, and the vehicle had no shock absorber.

Majid barely made it on time to the airport. By the time he got there, his head was pounding so hard that his vision became blurred. Yet, he was gratified by the prospects of leaving his homeland for good.

While at the airport, Majid picked up a local newspaper. Like other members of the lower class who spent a majority of their time worrying more about survival than contemporary issues, he was never a fan of the newspapers. Since, he was making a spirited transition to another part of the world, Majid felt like reading the local newspaper for a change. So, he bought a copy.

The headline news was in bold, flashy letters that practically jumped out of the newspaper. The Federal minister for transportation and road maintenance had been involved in a life threatening motor accident along the very major road he was contracted to modernize. For years, the honorable minister had received huge sums of money for that same road which had already exchanged hands between previous administrations. Yet, with inadequate gutters and drainage systems, the road remained littered with deepening pot holes and gullies that turned it into sequential death-traps for the road-users.

The honorable minister's driver was at top speed when the accident occurred. He was trying to avoid one of the numerous pot holes in a location known for incessant robbery when he veered off the road and collided with a trailer that had broken down on the road. The vehicle caught fire instantly killing the driver and the minster's body guard. Though the honorable minster was lucky to escape alive, he sustained multiple fractures and third degree burns on two thirds of his body.

As if to exacerbate the irony confronting the entire nation, the honorable minister's wife happened to be the immediate junior sister to the honorable minster for health. Unfortunately, there was no single health facility in the nation equipped to handle major accident victims.

News of the accident spread like wild fire and was everywhere; in the newspapers, on the television, in the radio. The entire nation was in a very somber mood and messages of hope and prayers were pouring in everywhere from the high and the mighty.

The airport was being readied for the immediate transportation of the wounded honorable minster to a foreign country by an air ambulance for proper treatment. As a result, *all* regular immigration and aviation activities at the international airport came to a virtual standstill.

One hour later, the paralysis of the international airport came to an abrupt end when the news filtered out that the honorable minster for transportation and road maintenance had expired. The mighty had fallen!

"The nation has lost an icon, an irreplaceable stalwart, a legend, an industrious son and one of the pillars of the land. The honorable minister for transportation and road maintenance has left behind a huge vacuum that cannot be filled," said a tearful government spokesman on the television screen.

It seemed the entire nation had *died* along with the honorable minister.

Majid matched the airport television announcement with his own thoughts--

"I am reminded of a story about a man who was taking refuge in the bush. When he discovered that goats were grazing in the same vicinity as his, he mowed down the entire grass. Subsequently, with nothing left to shield him from the scorching heat of sunshine, he became a victim of severe dehydration and sunburn.

Once in a while, the sadists are caught in the web of their own making.

As a proverb goes; 'A dog cannot run faster than its tail'. They steal the money meant for our roads. And, when they get involved in accidents, they head overseas. Sometimes, it's too little too late for survival.

They embezzle the money meant for our hospitals. And, when they are faced with medical and surgical emergencies, they head overseas. Sometimes, it's too late to get professional help.

They pocket the money meant for our academic institutions. And, when their kids grow up, they are sent to some of the best schools abroad. Sometimes, the kids are either lost to drugs, recklessness and criminality, or they refuse to come back to the same parents that sent them away.

In the words of the elders, 'the evil seed you plant as a child may produce the stump that will disable you later in life when you may think you have found peace'.

They steal public money to fortify themselves. They purchase bullet-proof vests, bullet-proof cars, bullet-proof windows; and they live in crime-proof houses with imposing gates, high-walled fences and steel metal protectors. Sometimes, security breaches still occur during which they become victims of the same broken system they had perpetuated.

In the words of the elders, 'when you break the plate you eat from, you start eating from the floor. And, every bite becomes a struggle with the sand'

Who thought that an honorable minster for transportation and road maintenance could die like a sacrificial lamb on the same road that filled his pockets with huge sums of embezzled money?

The man who deprived the goats of grazing grass has succumbed to the wrath of sunshine. The man who killed and buried integrity and honesty has been dragged down the grave by the same vices he nurtured.

In the words of the elders, 'No matter how high the cricket flies, it will fall down to be eaten by the toads' "

CHAPTER 6.

After the delay caused by the honorable minister's health and death issues, regular activities were resumed at the international airport at the usual snail pace. The line of passengers trying to check in their luggage was long, the process was painfully slow, and tempers were short. After what seemed like 'forever', it was Majid's turn to check in his lone luggage.

"*Open the luggage! What do you have there?*" a poker-faced ticket agent surrounded by stern-looking security men asked him.

"*The luggage contains only my clothes, and some processed foodstuff, sir,*" Majid replied politely.

"*You can't carry foodstuff out or this country. That is contraband*"

"*I didn't know that, sir*"

"*That will cost you two thousand in local currency*".

"*I didn't spend that much on the foodstuff, sir*"

"*I'm only trying to help you. If my superior sees the foodstuff, you won't even be allowed to travel at all. Pay the money before I change my mind*"

Majid remembered he had a few thousand of the local currency left in his pocket. Maybe he wouldn't need them in the United States after all.

"*O.K., sir, I will give you the money*".

"*Put it inside your passport and hand it to me. Don't let anybody see it*"

Ironically, everybody *saw* and *knew* what went on behind the check-in counter on a *daily* basis. What difference did it make? And, who cared, anyway?

Majid complied with the order. He didn't want anything to stop him from reaching the land of milk and honey.

Actually, there was *no law* prohibiting travelers from carrying processed foodstuffs out of the country. Rather, it was a country where 'laws' were repeatedly fabricated, *on the spot*, to suit individual purposes.

Majid heaved a sigh of relief as his lone luggage bounced down the conveyor belt, away from the counter.

"I don't have to deal with this stupid corrupt system anymore," he gloated.

He passed through customs and immigrations, having paid the airport tax. At the exit terminal, all the passengers were seated in one location, waiting to board the plane when an announcement was made over the loudspeaker:

"Every passenger must go downstairs and identify his or her luggage. No unidentified luggage will accompany passengers to New York"

A small dingy staircase led the passengers to an open, semi-lit field. There, all the passengers' bags and luggage were scattered haphazardly. Majid peeped into the partial darkness searching for his lone luggage. It was not so easy to distinguish one identical-looking luggage from another. When he found his luggage, he bent over to check the name tag. The luggage was his. He looked around, trying to figure out what next to do.

"Is that your luggage? Open it!"

Majid was startled by the order that seemed to come from nowhere. He searched his pockets for the keys as he looked in the direction of the voice.

Quickly, the luggage was flipped open.

"You have foodstuffs in there! It is contraband," the vague figure barked authoritatively, flashing his torchlight into the open luggage.

Majid didn't need any *further* instructions. He simply dipped his hand into the coat pocket and brought out whatever what left of the local currency. The money quickly exchanged hands.

He remembered the saying that *'palm wine poured on the floor is an invitation to the flies'.*

"*Traveling out of this country with foodstuff has quickly become 'an invitation to the flies'. Soon, no one can breathe in this land without giving a bribe,*" he lamented.

"*You can close your luggage. Have a safe journey, Sir. And, when you get there, don't forget those of us who are struggling here in this dry land of suffering*"

"*Thank you, Sir*"

"*First, they rob and milk you dry. Then, they wish you a safe journey. 'Don't forget those of us struggling here,' he says. You haven't started 'struggling' yet. Unless you change your ways in this country, you all will continue to struggle till the end of time,*" he said to himself.

Soon, Majid was back upstairs where the passengers were convinced they would *soon* be airborne. He wondered if his luggage would ever make it to New York, his final destination in America. Two *hours* later, there was no word on boarding; not even from the stone-faced airline agents lurking around aimlessly. It was getting dark, hot and sweaty, and the babies were beginning to wail freely in the open.

"*Maybe we won't even travel tonight,*" a frustrated female traveler lamented openly.

"*At least we have come this far,*" someone in the crowd replied, trying to look on the positive side.

"*Even if we have to sleep on the couch, we're among the lucky few,*" a third voice concurred.

"*This is a country where nothing works,*" a frustrated voice murmured with a sigh.

The only thing the passengers could do was to murmur and complain in groups of twos and threes as they sat and waited in silent disgust. One would expect an open revolt or some angry demands for better conditions. None was forthcoming. The people had become so *immune* to disappointments, abuses, and inhuman treatments that nothing seemed to faze them.

With no functioning air-conditioner, the room was so hot.

Several people scooped warm sweat from their glistening foreheads. Others fanned themselves, ineffectively, with tired open palms.

Then, suddenly, there was an announcement blared over the public speaker. It was time for boarding. The actual gate leading to the plane was still blocked with a metallic chain, and none of the airline agents was on hand.

The announcement precipitated a spontaneous stampede; a mad rush that seemed to energize the screaming babies. The only entrance to the plane was suddenly *clogged* with shoving humans. It was as if a thousand individuals were trying to squeeze through a rigid, frozen pathway; all at the same time.

Majid couldn't help thinking, once again, of the land and the people he was part of--

"We, the people; we will push and shove at every opportunity. One would think that the act of smooching bodies, and sharing other people's breadth and sweat brings us some type of exhilaration, or fulfillment. We fight so hard to get nowhere".

Then there was another announcement over the public speaker.

"Everybody should get seated. Only the pregnant women, the very old and disabled, and those with infants will board first".

Who was listening? It took repeated announcement to impress on the passengers that they were going nowhere. The struggle then shifted toward getting a seat *closest* to the boarding gate. There was the usual panting, and sweating.

Finally, an airline agent appeared, *in person*, and started checking in pregnant women, the very old and the young who were forced to squeeze through tight spots to board the plane.

One by one, *everyone* got into the plane, and no one was left behind. Every passenger took possession of the very seat allotted to him or her and there were empty seats as well!

Majid could not understand the *sense* in all the pushing and shoving to get into a half-empty plane with individually assigned seats.

He was about to sit down when a flamboyant passenger dressed in cowboy boots and hat tapped him on the shoulder.

"*What's up ma-men? Where'you going; ma-men?*"

"*I'm going to America,*" Majid replied, wondering why someone would address him as *'men'* instead of *'man'*.

"*Everybody's going to America. I mean what part of America?*" *the passenger asked him.*

"*Oh, I'm going to New York,*" Majid replied.

"*Ah! The Big Apple! Me, I'm going to Florida, the Sunshine State. Have a pleasant trip, ma-men! Perhaps, we'll meet again sometime, somewhere in America*"

With that, the 'Sunshine' man proceeded to his assigned seat at the rear end of the plane like a professional traveler.

After fitting his hand luggage in the overhead compartment Majid squeezed himself into the segmented little space which would serve as his 'bedroom' for the length of the journey. The passenger on his left was flabby, and too close for comfort. Majid felt like a claustrophobic whose little space had been violated by an alien. In addition, his legs were simply too long for the short space in front of him.

Luckily, on the other side of him was the window. That provided some reprieve, and a chance to look away from his flabby neighbor and embrace the beauty of the uninhibited, naked skies.

He went into a reflective mood; something that had become his trademark--

"*Wow! I feel like a bird that has been released from a cage. Is this what freedom feels like?*

The sky is magnificent in its beauty and I'm privileged to embrace it! Is this what freedom feels like?

It is limitless, it is profound, it is exhilarating and it is calm.

I have tested freedom on the wings of an airplane. Now, it's time for me to develop my own wings and fly like a bird.

CHAPTER 7.

On arrival at the Kennedy International airport, Majid followed the 'exit' sign along with other passengers. After going through the immigration, a remarkably smooth process compared to his experience back home, the young man collected his lone luggage and walked into a large crowd of people who were anxiously waiting to receive passengers from different flights. His was only one of several flights arriving at an airport where planes were landing and departing few *minutes* apart.

Among the large crowd, he saw his countryman, the 'Good Samaritan', holding a sign bearing his name in bold letters. There were other people holding similar signs with different names.

Majid went straight to the 'Good Samaritan'.

"Good day Sir. My name is Majid," he said as the man shook his hand.

"My brother, welcome to America. My name is Tutu," the man responded.

"Thank you, sir"

"Don't call me 'Sir'. Here in America, there is no need for that. My name is Tutu"

"Yes uncle"

After all the introduction, hugs and handshake, it was time for Majid to be driven to his new temporary home in America.

Since he arrived at the airport, he had felt like someone in a different planet. Everything was *different* in a superior sense.

"I'm very grateful for your kindness, uncle"

"Relax. There's plenty of hard work ahead of you"

Like most of the vehicles at the airport parking lot, Tutu's car looked and smelt like it was brand new. That was quite unlike a majority of the vehicles seen on the roads back home.

When Majid sat on the fluffy comfortable cushion, he felt like royalty. Everything had a touch of luxury-the silent air conditioner, the beautiful sound system, the fresh-minty smell; even the majestic interior.

It was a very *smooth* ride through the highway with no checkpoints manned by gun trotting, bribe-soliciting policemen; no gaping potholes, no precipitous land erosions, and no abandoned vehicles. The few houses visible from the roadside were devoid of cracks, decay and sheets of brown dust.

They stopped by a restaurant where a waiter ushered them in to a clean table set for two people. The tablecloth, napkins, glasses and cutlery were freshly cleaned, and well arranged. Each of them was handed a menu.

"You choose whatever you want to eat," Tutu told Majid.

"I'm not too familiar with some of the dishes," Majid confessed.

"Don't worry, brother. I'll order for you," Tutu volunteered.

"You can try a little bit of salad, sirloin steak and French fries. You'll like it"

"But, uncle, can't we order something cheaper?" Majid asked, looking at the prices.

"Settle down first. Then, you'll have more than your share of cheap food".

Majid liked the food. It tasted great. But, he thought it was too much food for *one* person. The steak was more than enough meat for a family back home. When he looked around and saw what other customers had on their plates, Majid was amazed that people could eat so much food at a time.

Suddenly, he remembered what a fellow hawker had said to him on the eve of his departure from home--

"Watch what you eat, brother, when you get there. Remember the saying: 'I'll rather go hungry than black out from bulimia'. America is a land of fattening, junk food. You are going to see lots of people with

bulging stomach hanging out like accessory organs. These are the same people who'll swear they never eat a full meal".

Majid had never seen people eat so much meat and fish in *one* meal. The steak came in big, juicy slices. The food tasted so good he couldn't care whether it was 'fattening' or not. Didn't our people say that *'something that is good is worth treating well?'* The food was great, and he simply did justice to it.

"If one dies eating like this, something good will come out of it. The taste buds will definitely smile from here to eternity!" he thought.

Tutu ordered red wine for himself and a medium size Coke for Majid; the soft drink that was very ubiquitous back home.

"If this bucket is 'medium' size, I wonder what 'large' size will look like," Majid joked in his mind.

The young man ate so much food that his body suddenly became stiff. His could hardly breathe. It was a meal to remember, and cherish; his first great meal in America.

"Thank you, uncle," he greeted Tutu.

"It's my pleasure, brother," Tutu replied.

It was time for Desert. Tutu ordered cheesecake.

"What do you want for Desert, brother?" Tutu asked.

Majid took a long, deep breadth like one caught in a dilemma.

"I ate so much already I think I am going to explode. Besides, people like me don't eat dessert back home," he replied.

"Well, I can't force you. If you change your mind, let me know"

"Yes uncle".

Majid's mind wondered back to the country he came from--

"Back home, we have a problem; we starve from lack of food. Down here, they have a problem; they explode from too much of it. If each side could only give some of their problem to the other, the world would be a better place for all".

He thought of his late parents. One died in jail for a debt he could never pay back on time. The other died from lack of medical attention. He had no siblings to worry about.

His thoughts shifted toward *death* and its after-effects--

"Death, with all your callousness, you do have a fair side as well. You treat everybody the same way and bring absolute equality to mankind.

Death, with all your brutality, you do have a kind face as well. My mother could have been alive today. Yet, you liberated her from the constant agony of hunger, want and deprivation.

Death, with all your cold-heartedness, you do have a soft side as well. My father could have been alive today. Yet, you freed him from constant harassment, worries and lack of sleep.

Death, with all your inclemency, you do have a sunny side as well. Today, deprived of parents and siblings, I'm like a millipede. Anywhere I die becomes my home. I don't have to worry about a sick mother, a struggling father or desperate siblings begging for help.

With my parents gone and well-rested in the land of the dead, I can now concentrate on my fight against poverty".

(PART TWO: THE END).

CHAPTER 1.

As soon as they arrived at the apartment, Tutu laid down the rules which Majid must follow. Majid could stay for as long as his visa was valid but not beyond the expiration date. He could look for some odd jobs to make some money. He must stay out of trouble at all times. And, if he should commit any crime, he would be entirely on his own.

Two days later, Majid came across two youngsters who were arguing on the street. One of them was brandishing a handgun threatening to kill the other. Majid stepped in between the boys to prevent a deadly act. Back home in the village, he would feel *obligated* to do exactly the same thing.

The two wrangling individuals were utterly stunned that a *total* stranger could risk his life so foolishly for something that didn't even concern him. The armed man balked at firing the gun, stepped backward and lowered his hand.

"What? Who is this clown? You have to be stupid, insane or mentally-retarded to step in front of someone with a gun! Oh; I see it! You look like someone from the jungle where bullets don't scare anybody," he addressed a totally-confused Majid who could hardly understand what the armed man was saying in his hippy accent.

"And you; did you pay this moron to stick his head out and die for you? Trust me; there'll be another day, another place and another time," he warned his equally stupefied foe as he walked away without firing a bullet.

When Majid got home and told his host about the encounter he had with the two youngsters, he was rebuked severely for putting his life at risk.

"You must count yourself lucky to be still alive! The next time you act this stupid, you'll find yourself out in the street. 'It is when a mad man is killed that his kinsmen will come to light'. The moment you die, all those relatives of yours who never existed in your time of need, will surface and accuse me of sacrificing your worthless body for ritual purposes!"

Majid couldn't help wondering why city life could be so *different* from that in the village where he came from--

"We are same humanity; yet we are so different.

Back in the village, every child is everybody's child; every parent is everybody's parent; every sibling is everybody's sibling. Here, in the city, it's all different. Here, everybody is on his or her own.

We are same people; yet we are so different.

Back in the village, when one person dies, the whole community mourns; when one person smiles, everybody smiles along and when sorrow visits one person, everybody feels the heat. Here, in the city, it's all different. Here, everybody lives in his or her own separate and isolated world.

Back in the village, we fight with soft knuckles and harmless objects. And, when one sees a gun, it looks more like a toy; a relic than a common weapon. Here, it's all different. Here in the city, guns seem to be everywhere, and when people fight with guns, it looks more like routine than exceptional.

Back in the village, we know each other's business and we mediate in times of conflict and misunderstanding. Here, it's all different. Here in the city, solitude rather than engagement is the rule of common sense".

He had already learnt one important lesson about his new surrounding; to stay *clear* of other people's business.

Majid quickly inquired about odd-job openings; those low-paying menial jobs that could be obtained 'illegally'. The payment was usually made in cash or 'under the table' as it was commonly described. The 'employee' would take his or her money home without paying any taxes.

Someone told him there were such jobs available; if only he was *willing and able* to work hard. He could pump gas at the gas station, take a security job, work for a professional mover, (where he must move heavy objects from one location to another), deliver newspapers (on a bicycle), or simply attach himself to a painter, a plumber or a landscaper for a couple bucks a day. The prospects of finding a job filled him with great hope and excitement.

Quickly, he started going from one job to another.

First, he joined a mover. He had no problem finding such a job. All he needed was his strength and the willingness to work hard. The first day, they moved *every* equipment and furniture in some business office from one floor to the one above it. The following morning, he could not *raise* his hand enough to comb my hair. The muscles were stiff, the legs were numb, and he had stomach spasms. He simply ached all over. He quickly abandoned that job and even *cursed* his 'employer' for being so 'wicked'.

Then, he took a job pumping gas at a gas station for an individual owner. It was in the middle of *winter*, and he didn't have a warm winter jacket. His plan was to buy one with his first 'paycheck'. He survived the very first day by wearing several layers of clothing, blowing hot breath, repeatedly, into his bare hands and shaking different parts of the body to create heat.

The following day was *awfully* cold. He was pumping gas when a fly flew straight to his face. Instinctively, he slapped the right ear in an attempt to kill or chase away the fly. He felt *nothing*; not even the forceful impact of his palm. That was rather strange. He slapped himself again; this time *purposely*. Again, he felt nothing, absolutely nothing! That was when he decided to *pinch* what used to be his right ear; then the left one. There was *no* feeling in either of the auricles.

"What happened to my ears?" he asked himself; his heart skipping a few quick beats.

He wanted to say something. He couldn't. Like rigid frozen parts, the quivering lips refused to part. That was when he left the customer in a hurry and ran to the bathroom. He was still in the process of filling up a customer's fuel tank when the incident occurred. When he got to the bathroom, he went straight to the mirror and looked at his ears. Both ears were still in place; *intact*. He tugged on both ears and pinched them very hard. He felt *nothing*; not even a tingle.

Meanwhile, impatient customers were blowing their horns outside, demanding quicker service. Through his frozen lips and chattering teeth, Majid *cursed* them and *cursed* the man that employed him as he practically fled the scene and ran back to the apartment as fast as his legs could carry him. People must have thought he was a lunatic; or someone being chased by the devil.

By the time he got to the apartment, Majid had generated enough body heat to regain *some* of his body sensations. Sweating, he was partly warm and partly numb. He felt odd like a frozen mummy being thawed, rather slowly. Good a thing, he did not use hot water to hasten the "thawing process".

"It is so true that 'the sheep which must grow horns must have a thick skull'. Success never comes easy," he murmured.

From that very day, the mere *thought* of a gas station sent shivers down his spine.

Four weeks had already passed by, and he was beginning to get frustrated. Winter was still raging. It was chilly, frosty, messy and nasty. One day, at the end of a horrific blizzard, he saw a couple of young men passing through the neighborhood with shovels in their hands. He wondered what could make them leave their homes in such terrible weather. When he found out that the young men were making *money* digging out snow from people's driveways and the surrounding sidewalks, he borrowed a shovel from Uncle Tutu and joined them.

He came back with more money than he had ever made in one day! From that day, each time there was a blizzard, he would walk around with a shovel and come home smiling. The winter season provided him with a steady flow of untaxed income.

Life, so far had been harsh. But, nothing in his newly-adopted land would compare with the hell his homeland had been for him.

No one in America had ever splashed him with filthy water

mixed with human waste. No one had flogged him with a horsewhip. No one had arrested and jailed him with false charges. No one had treated him like a useless object.

He couldn't help being philosophical--

"That, which makes one man smile, can bring tears of sorrow to another.

Sometimes, when an association benefits one and damages the other, they call it parasitism.

Back home, the sadists smile on our backs while we toil and sweat in agony.

That, which is repugnant to one person, can be an amiable lifesaver for another.

Sometimes, when there is discord or lack of agreement between parties, they call it disharmony.

The same jobs that are hated and rejected by the indigenes are the ones which the immigrants embrace with gratitude.

The same jobs that bring stress, sadness and a sense of discrimination to the indigenes are the ones that bring peace, happiness, and a sense of belonging to the immigrants.

The same jobs that wear down the indigenes are the ones that bring strength and vigor to the immigrants.

That, which brings two dissimilar individuals together, can be beneficial to both.

Sometimes, when there is a mutually-beneficial relationship between different people or groups, they call it symbiosis.

On the surface, the indigenes and immigrants seem at odds with each other; yet they are so interdependent.

The immigrants build and cater for the indigenes while the indigenes sustain the hope of the needy immigrants.

Individually, they falter, and decay. Yet, together, they succeed and prosper in more ways than one.

CHAPTER 2.

"Uncle, when was the last time you visited home and why are you still single?" Majid asked Tutu one beautiful evening.

They had just finished dinner and were relaxing in the living room. The two had formed a habit of having a nice conversation after dinner.

"To answer that question, I'd have to tell you the entire history of my life abroad," Tutu replied.

"Hmm," Majid responded with expression of regret for asking the question.

"Don't get me wrong. You asked a very good question. Sharing the story of my life with someone like you is something that has become part of my mission," Tutu reassured him.

"I didn't mean to violate your private life, Uncle".

"No, you're not violating my private life. Right now, I have all the time to share my story with you. Perhaps, you'll learn something useful listening to me.

On the eve of my departure from home, my mother, who was alive by then, spoke and acted very much like one whose son was being sent the gallows:

"Son, look at me, your mother. In just a few short hours, they will take you away from me. Will I see you again? Please, promise me that I will see you again. 'When a child begins to learn how to climb trees, the mother begins to learn how to cry'. You are suddenly growing up and that scares me. You know how home is. If you go there and disgrace us, you will never see my face again. I will kill myself for you. I hear

50

so many bad things about that place. You remember my nephew, Simba, how he used to be the pride of the land.

The first time he came back from America, he was spending money like it was cocoyam leaf, and he was so generous to everybody.

During his second visit, the traditional ruler bestowed upon him a befitting chieftaincy title. At that ceremony, Simba presented his fiancée to the community. She was a beautiful medical doctor and daughter of a reputable community leader from a neighboring village. The ovation, which Simba received at that ceremony, was deafening, long and lasting.

His third and final visit home was for the traditional wedding ceremony; an event that brought out the low and the mighty alike. After that ceremony, Simba left the village to return to America.

Then, like one swallowed by time, he vanished from the land that harbored his placenta-- no letters, no communication, no more visits, nothing! If his parents were alive today, they would have both committed suicide.

Please my son; don't let America swallow you alive like it swallowed my nephew. *'When an eagle begins to feed on corpses, it has problem distinguishing itself from the vulture'.* If you go there and follow some people to act stupid, all of you will be grouped together; and what happens to stupid people will happen to you. *'A poor man's fowl is his cow'.* You are all I have. We may not be rich or prominent in the society, yet I am satisfied with what I have. *'The sole palm seed held in the mouth of a squirrel prevents it from opening the mouth wide'.* I can't gamble with your life. If you get lost, who will give me another son? *'My name doesn't sound well when it is whispered'.* Please don't do anything that will make people whisper my name and give it a bad meaning. Don't worry about me here. I will be fine. I don't want money, or material things from you. All I want is a good son who will come back to his ailing mother, alive and well, and make me proud. May the road protect you; my son. You must write home very often. If I don't hear from you, I will fall sick. I wish your father had been alive today. Each time I look at you, I see your father in you. *'A good tree bears good fruits'.* You are a good man; like your father was. The task you have chosen, that of going abroad, is not going to be an easy one. But then, *'the luggage you personally place on your own head will not crush you'.* You took up this task on your own and it will not overcome you. *'It's one finger that dips the palm oil which lubricates the entire hand'.* Whatever you bring home, whether it is shame or good fortune, will affect the entire village. Bring back good fortune; not shame. Should something happen to me while you are there, you must remain strong; and carry on, like a man. That is all I have to say. *'The toad says that too much water in the ditch does not allow it to croak'.* I'm too overwhelmed to speak any further. May the land and air protect you; my son".

That was my mother then.

When I came to America, I saw myself as someone representing my village back home. I saw myself as 'my village' in America. I was my village and if I succeeded, that village would have succeeded. If I failed, the village would have failed automatically. I wasn't going to travel thousands of miles and degrade, debase, shame, humiliate or misrepresent my proud and honorable family; or the same village I had come to personify. I worked hard, did my school work and stayed out of trouble. I wanted to please my mother and make her proud.

One day, I got carried away by the glamour and opportunities presented by the American system. I joined the wrong group. One thing led to another and I quickly postponed my lofty objectives and started skipping classes. It is said that *'when an animal falls into a trap, the proposed journey comes to an end'.* I fell off the cliff and lost my lofty objectives.

My travails deepened when I decided to get married. I wanted to marry a girl from home and I specifically told them to find me a registered nurse; someone who would come here and make plenty of money for me. In order to impress the girl they found for me, I lied to her about all the education and wealth I had acquired in America. I don't know if she fell for my lies, or if she had her own ulterior motives. I went home and married her in an elaborate traditional ceremony. I made my mother very proud. She gave us her blessings and wanted us to give her lots of grandchildren. When my wife came here, she mellowed down, and acted like a naïve and obedient village girl. It is said that *'when the fire bows to the wind, it appears to be dead'.* My wife was neither naïve nor gullible. She was busy *doing her homework. At the appropriate time, she divorced me and took me to the cleaners. I was totally humiliated. If I hadn't been patient and tolerant enough, the relationship would have resulted in homicide.*

After the divorce, everything seemed to work against me. I lost my regular security job, and jumped from one menial job to another; the only type of job I could get without a college degree. My problems were compounded when my mother died and I could not go home to bury her.

Years later, I decided to clean my acts. That was when I took a decision to acquire something which I could someday call my own-- a degree, a house, a business; something. So, I decided to save some money and build an average size house in the village where I might 'retire' in my old age. Though my parents were both deceased, my senior brother was alive and well in the village. I sent him money to purchase a good piece of land and start building a suitable house for me. I also sent him a building plan of the type of house I wanted. From all indications, he simply carried out my instructions to the letter and sent me photographs and updates on the new house.

One day, I got a letter from my senior brother. The house had been completed. He wanted me to send money for furniture, appliances, and various other fixtures. That was when I decided to take a temporary leave from the hustle and bustle of the American life and visit home for the second time. I had to get away for a while from the hell I was in.

It is said that 'one, who has not been to the war front, sees war as a wrestling match'. I hadn't been home for a long time so I miscalculated the level of hardship involved in my second journey home. There were so many obstacles facing me-- the cost of travel, the burden of excess luggage, the temporary loss of income, and the additional, unavoidable expenses back home. In addition, I had to endure lengthy sleep deprivation, unpredictable flight schedules, harassment from immigration authorities, risky travel by land, and invasion of privacy by home folks. I had used my credit cards to borrow money at high interest rate for the journey.

In anticipation for a potential barrage of questions concerning my wife and children, I drilled myself with questions and answers.

I was going to lie to the people and paint a rosy picture of my perfect marriage in America. Which one of them would come here to establish the truth?

When I got home, the first person I met was my senior brother. We exchanged the usual greetings, and went through a question-and-answer session.

"Is that you, my brother? You're home safely. We thank God".

"I'm so glad to be home, brother. It has been such a long and tedious journey. How is everybody?"

"We have all dried up here like stockfish, my brother".

"Where are the children?"

"Children? They are no longer children. They have all graduated from the University and gone their separate ways. It's just me, my wife and 'little Tiger' left behind here in the village".

"You're not doing badly at all, my brother. All your children except 'little Tiger' have graduated from the University? That is a great achievement"

"How is your wife in America? How many children do you have now? Husband and wife; one is a super graduate, the other a registered nurse. You must be living big in America"

'When an insect is frying, they say it is looking fresh and well oiled,' I thought.

"Brother, life in America is not as good as it is perceived by folks back home," I replied.

"In the words of the elders, 'even if you give a man the whole world, he will never be satisfied with what he has'. How can someone living big in America come home to this dry land and complain? Look at those shoes and the jeans you're wearing. It has always been my dream to wear stuff like that," he said.

"Well, brother, it's no longer a dream. I will leave them behind for you and much more. Where's my house? I want to unpack my luggage"

"You'll leave those shoes and jeans for me? That's nice of you. It's true that 'one who has someone in heaven does not go to hell'. It was just last week I attended this wedding ceremony. Everyone was wearing a watch except me. Life can be cruel!" he exclaimed, fixing his eyes on my watch as he spoke. His intentions were unmistakable.

"Well, brother, this time around you're going to get your own watch".

"Isn't that very kind of you? May I never lack a brother like you! Tell me about your beautiful wife. How is she, and how many children do you have now?"

"My wife is just fine. We have two children; a boy and a girl"

"You had two children and we never knew anything about them? Why didn't you bring them along?"

"Maybe next time, I will bring them with me"

"It's good to hear that all is well with you and your family in America. It's said that 'an adult pretends to scratch his behind when he is actually passing gas'. If I didn't know you well as a brother, I would have thought that your wife divorced you and you came home with a bunch of lies to fool those of us who can't board an airplane; the type of story one would expect from the white man's land"

I was caught off guard by those comments. My heart skipped a few quick beats.

'Hm! I wonder how much this man knows about my life in America!' I thought.

"Where is my house? I need to rest a little, and unpack my luggage," I asked, trying to change the subject quickly.

"Stay in my house for now. We'll talk about your house tomorrow. Your children, what are their names? I cant' wait to see their photographs"

"After a very long journey, I could use a glass of wine and get some rest. Is my house far away from here?" I asked desperately, struggling to change the subject.

"You certainly need some rest, brother. You know how inquisitive our people are. By the time you're through with the family, your in-laws, your age group, not to talk of the entire community, you'll need more than a glass of wine".

"Why should I even care about the inquisitiveness of the community and the in-laws right now? What I need is rest more than anything else," I responded.

"You should care. In the words of the elders, 'he who brings an ant-infested faggot into his house should not complain when lizards begin to pay him a visit'.

It is only when you have something to hide that you'll worry about unwelcome company".

The man's comments were as biting as they were judgmental. I could feel my defense mechanisms crumbling as fast as I felt the heat from within.

"I'm not yet settled and this man is already dissecting me!" I thought.

I tried to force a change in the subject matter.

"This is a beautiful house you have here, brother. You know, few people can afford a house like this in America," I complimented him.

"You Americans, you always complain, even if your wealth is flowing like the village river. It is said that 'a person with good legs does not know what a cripple goes through' How long are you staying?"

"Now he's pushing me to get nasty. Then, people will say I'm disrespecting my senior brother". I said to myself as I tried to remain calm.

"I will be home for three weeks," I replied.

"Three weeks must be the lucky number for you folks over there. Every one of you who visits home will hurry back at the end of three weeks".

"God, give me the strength to stay calm!" I screamed in my mind.

"Frankly speaking, I will like to get into my own house now and relax. Where is your wife?" I responded with apparent anger.

"My wife? She went to the market. If you see her carrying her empty basket to the market, you'll think she is making money. She should be back soon"

"I'm so exhausted I'll like to enter my own house and get some rest," I practically commanded him.

My senior brother responded in kind.

"Since you came back here, all you've been talking about is 'my house; my house'. There are plenty of rooms in this house for you to settle down and unpack your Oyibo luggage! And, besides, there are more important issues for you to worry about than your stupid house," he exploded in my face.

It is said that 'the ominous drums of war are silent until someone strikes them'.

My senior brother suddenly sounded like the sleeping drums of warfare that had been awaken by my presence. I wondered if he was the same senior brother I had left at home, and if it had become a crime to inquire about one's own house. I couldn't hide my anger and bewilderment any more.

"What exactly is going on here? Are you not happy to see me, or something? I spent days traveling home only to be treated like an unwanted guest by my own blood brother. Should I wait for your wife to come home and take me to my own house?" I finally yelled back at my senior brother.

"You're not home quite twenty minutes and you already want my wife to follow you to your house. 'Any ant dipped into a pot of oil can never come out unsoiled'. You're acting like an ant that's already deep inside a pot of oil and it's beginning to show," he screamed back at me.

"Right now, I feel like a rat surrounded by traps. I think I'll go and sleep in a hotel," I snarled back; no longer able to keep my emotions in check.

"It is said that 'only a child sees a scorpion and calls it a grasshopper'. If I were you, I wouldn't make such a foolish decision. Hotels are not safe in this part of the world. They say that 'a stray chick ready to be carried away by the hawk should first be saved. Then, the chick can be scolded for not watching its steps'. I feel obligated to safeguard your life right now before you do something stupid. It is said that 'If a fowl pollutes the air, it starts running even when nobody is seen chasing it'. You make me wonder if something is chasing you away from your father's compound".

He was brutally cynical.

I felt like someone who was about to explode. I thought of the constant hell I had been through in America over the years. Was this the same senior brother who was supposed to be taking care of the home front? I was completely at a loss. I felt various emotions sweeping through my system in rapid succession-- from bewilderment to sadness to bitterness to remorse to self-pity to anger and confusion.

"It is said that 'Loud gas sounds better when it is passed by the king'. If I treated you the way you are treating me right now, everybody would

condemn me. They say 'you can't beat a child and stop him from crying'. That is what you're trying to do to me," I told him.

At this juncture, my senior brother simply walked away without saying another word.

"I remembered what the elders had said: 'The evil seed you plant as a child may produce the stump that will disable you later in life when you may think you have found peace'. And, again; 'when an elder plants a breadfruit tree on a busy family road, the fruit of that tree will someday fall down and kill that elder, or one of his children'.

I wondered if one or both of us had already sowed the evil seed without knowing it".

CHAPTER 3.

Uncle Tutu continued the story of his life as Majid sat patiently listening with a keen interest.

"I was standing there contemplating my next move when my brother's wife suddenly came back from the market carrying a basket on her head".

"Thank goodness you're back, my brother's wife. I was told you went to the market," I greeted her with indifference and residual anger.

The woman looked at me rather curiously; the same way one would look at a total stranger.

"It's me, Tutu. I'm back from America," I reminded her.

"Oh, I didn't even recognize you. You're not dried up like the rest of us here at home. For a minute there, I was wondering what someone from a better world should be doing in this dry land of ours".

"It's said that 'One can tell a ripe corn by looking at it'. Everybody at home has indeed turned into a dried stockfish," I replied, sarcastically.

"They say that 'when the pocket runs out of money the mouth runs out of smiles'. We don't even know how to smile anymore," she fired back.

"This woman's tongue is as sharp as her husband's," I said to myself.

"It is said that 'those who climb with their teeth know the taste of bitter trees'. You sound very much like your husband. Indeed, both of you must have tasted hardships together," I responded in kind.

"Have you already met him?" she asked.

"Yes. He told me you went to the market"

"It's market without money. We just go there to pass time. Why are you standing there? Come inside the house, and relax. I like that your luggage. I have always dreamt of having a luggage like that. I hope you'll leave it behind for me. I'm sure you brought us lots of good things from America"

"Your dream of having a luggage has come true. I'll leave it for you".

"Eh? You mean I'm going to have my own luggage? It's true that 'one, who has someone, is greater than the person who has money'. Thank you very much".

"It's my pleasure".

At that point in time, I thought it was better to keep silent and go inside the house before I would open another can of worms. The elders were right--'That I am silent does not mean I don't know what to say'. There was so much I could say to her but I chose to remain silent. It is said that 'one knowingly falls for laughter; that laughter does not push anybody down'. I followed her, willingly, into the house.

The house was moderately furnished, and fitted with modern conveniences. That was precisely the type of house I had instructed my senior brother to build for me, and it looked exactly like the one I saw in the pictures that were sent to me while I was in America. My stomach suddenly went into spasms and my chest began to hurt.

"How is America?" the woman asked, rather casually.

"America is there. How are things at home?" I responded.

"There's nothing here but hunger, and hardship. Look at us. We have all dried up like stockfish".

"It's so true! Things are so bad here that even the whales are beginning to dry up," I responded.

I couldn't have been more sarcastic. The woman, undoubtedly obese by modern standards, could benefit a lot from weight loss.

What had come over the folks back home? I had no one to confide in, so I kept every thought of mine to myself--

"I'm not home quite one hour and they have already shared me from head to toe. The only thing left of me is a walking image. They want the cheap watch I am wearing. They want the shoes I bought on sale. They want my recycled luggage. They want my ragged jeans. They want to have 'all the goods things' I brought home from

America. I bet they'll love to see me travel back naked and 'dried up' like the real stockfish. In the words of the elders, *'it's those yams belonging to a fool that are used to prepare the communal soup'. My cheap belongings have become public property".*

I kept my thoughts within me as I dropped my luggage and sank into the nearest chair, not sure what to do next.

"You can stay in one of the bedrooms upstairs. The rooms are not as comfortable as what you have there in America. It's just a place to stretch a tired body at the end of a penniless day," my brother's wife instructed me.

I followed her instructions and went upstairs to one of the bedrooms without saying a word. The room was far better and more comfortable than the dingy basement apartment I worked so hard to keep in America.

I remembered our deceased parents. If only they were alive! I lay down in bed, closed my eyes, and quickly went to sleep more from exhaustion than from lack of sleep.

I had barely slept for ten minutes when I felt a stiff finger poking me by the sides. I woke up with a jerk and a terrible headache!

"Welcome back, Uncle! Welcome back! Mama says I should come and get you. It's time to eat. The food is downstairs"

That was 'little Tiger' who had just come home after playing soccer with children his age.

"No, thanks, I'm not hungry. Hey, Tiger! You're such a big boy now! We should start calling you 'big Tiger'. Come and give Uncle a hug".

We hugged each other.

"Uncle, you're not hungry? Is it because Mama says you eat leaves and white man's food over there? You can at least manage what we have here. What did you bring for me, Uncle?"

"Listen Tiger, over there, we eat the same food you eat here; that is when we are lucky enough to find it. Do you know where your father built my house?"

"This is the only house Papa has built. He always says you'll build your own house if you ever come back"

"If I ever come back?"

"Everybody says that those of you in America will never come back here to settle down"

"Everybody says that?"

"Yes. They say you can only visit, and when you do, you usually run out of money in three weeks and then hurry back to pay your bills. That is why everybody tries to get what they can before other people grab it from you"

"Why does everybody want something from us?"

"Oh, you make plenty of money in America. Uncle Hill says he wears his old clothes whenever his little brother visits home from America so that he can get more out of him. He says he always welcomes his brother with a long list of problems".

"You know, Tiger, life can be more difficult in America than it is here at home".

"O no, it can't! They say that you guys say such things to deceive us. If America is that bad why don't you come back home and dry up like the rest of us here?"

"Tiger, 'it's not everything a palm wine tapper sees up there that he climbs down to narrate'. It's enough to say that life is very difficult abroad and people back home make it hard for those of us, returnees, to achieve anything useful".

"Everybody says you guys are good at giving orders; those of you in America--"Do this! Do that!" and that because you have dollars, you think you're doing better than everybody else at home".

"On the contrary, most of us in America will love to exchange places with folks back home. Look at my age mates; most of their children have graduated from the University. How many folks back home have experienced the stress of living in a foreign land? How many of them have been humiliated and insulted abroad for being different from others? How many bills do they receive in a month? Do they understand what it means to be a foreigner in a foreign land? Most of them live in the village where they don't have to worry about house rents and mortgages. How many of them get kicked out of their houses by spouses of many years? Have they ever experienced immigration problems? They can only hear stories of the extreme weather conditions that have become part of our daily lives abroad. We can't afford to have babies, like they do. Here, *some people have ten babies, and they don't have to worry about medical bills, baby sitters, and numerous baby needs. We can't afford to get sick, either. Here, in minor cases, they can get by with simple homemade remedies. They don't go to bed worrying about creditors and collection agencies. When we do go to bed at all, it is to fight insomnia and distress over money problems, job insecurity, deadlines, and numerous discriminative practices against us. Here, they take their sweet time to eat homemade meals; oblivious to the passage of time. For us, when we do eat at all, we must sometimes eat inside the car. We grab our cold food with one hand, and grip the steering wheel with the other. Half-chewed, the food is swallowed in lumps and in a hurry. That's the type of life we live in a foreign land. Then we visit home, only to be greeted with envy, jealousy and mischief!"*

Suddenly, I realized that I was verbalizing my pent-up feelings to a little boy. I had been carried away by my emotions.

"Uncle, you don't seem to like America very much. But, everybody here likes America and wants to go there".

"May their dreams come true, Amen!"

"Oh, what am I doing having such an adult discussion with a small boy? I must be going crazy!" I screamed in my mind.

Then, I remembered the saying: 'the mouse that ate my corn should not shower me with the particles'. My brother had taken away my house and I didn't think it was proper for him and his family to humiliate me as well. It is said that 'a person does not get lost when his or her thing gets lost'. I had already lost my house and my dignity. The least I could do was to pull myself together, like a man and avoid getting lost as well.

"Hey Tiger, go down and eat. Tell your mother I'm too tired, and that I'm not hungry. I need to get some rest," I told him gently. He was just a small boy. What did he know?

As soon as he left the room, I lay down on my back and supported the posterior part of my head with two hands clasped together. I stared at the ceiling. The ceiling stared back at me. That was when my senior brother's comments sank in and started to haunt me--

"If I didn't know you well as a brother, I would have thought that your wife divorced you and you came home with a bunch of lies to fool those of us who can't board an airplane; the type of story

one would expect from the white man's land'---'You certainly need some rest, brother. You know how inquisitive our people are. By the time you're through with the family, your in-laws, your age group, not to talk of the entire community, you'll need more than a glass of wine".

I could not help asking myself some questions. How much did the folks back home know about my life in America? Had my exwife been communicating with someone, or some people back home? Had I walked into a big trap? What did the family, the in-laws, the age group and the entire community have in store for me that my brother was talking about? I felt uneasy; and unsettled.

The following day, I left the house first thing in the morning before daybreak. Everybody was still asleep when I left the village. I didn't want to find out what was in store for me. I simply left everything behind--the entire luggage, the cheap watch, the ragged jeans, and the various gifts I had purchased in America. My senior brother had already swallowed years of my earnings and livelihood. I had been 'shared' from head to toe; what else was left of me? I could not leave my shoes behind; I had to walk on something. I could not leave the underwear, the shirt or my secondary cheap pair of trousers either. I had to wear something on my way back to America. Only lunatics were expected to travel around naked. Besides, I did not want to be labeled insane. That would give every 'dry stockfish' in the village something to gossip about.

"Maybe I should go back to America, buy me a cheap gun, and kill myself!" I murmured in disgust.

I knew I could never kill myself. No one in my family, or the entire village, had ever committed suicide. I wasn't going to be the first person to do so.

It is said that 'even when the wound heals; the scar remains'. I came back to America with a scar that refused to go away. As if the gods and humans had teamed up against me, I started going from one financial problem to another.

First, I lost my regular security job; and without a college degree, my search for a replacement job was futile. Then, numerous creditors came after me for a mountain of unpaid bills. I could no longer cope with my situation.

It is said that 'the fowl retires for the night, not because the stomach is full but because darkness has blocked its view'. I was forced to retire from all public events. During my better days, I would crisscross various States and attend weekend and night parties without reservation. It is said that 'the same raging fire that wrecks havoc will burn itself out'. I had extinguished myself after years of unrestrained recklessness. I could no longer afford to fuel and maintain a troubled used car; not to talk of money for public transportation. I solicited help from my numerous friends. Initially, the response was satisfactory. Then my friends, sensing that I had nothing to offer, began to avoid me; and finally they withered away. They stopped communicating with me, and even when I left messages on their answering machines, they would not return my calls.

A proverb says that 'when one begins to tap palm wine, one begins to tap the neighbors as well'. In the good olden days, I had a countless number of so-called friends who flocked endlessly around me just to satisfy their various needs. I was invited to every party in town. As soon I went belly up, the neighbors vanished from my sight. I had become a loser, a pariah; someone who had nothing to offer. 'When pride takes the lead, wealth takes a leave'. The moment I took pride in poor judgment and reckless lifestyle, success took a leave from me.

I thought of moving to a different State where nobody would know me; where I would simply blend away like a chameleon. Then, I remembered the words of my late mother--

"Please son, don't let America swallow you alive like it swallowed my nephew"----"When an eagle begins to feed on corpses, it has problem distinguishing itself from the vulture". If you go there and follow some people to act stupid, all of you will be grouped together; and what happens to stupid people will happen to you"

I started crying. How could I have forgotten those words so quickly?

I was once again invigorated. I disowned bad company, and I went back to school. In addition, I decided to help needy immigrants *like you to get on their feet. That was my way of making amends for disobeying my mother.*

You know how our parents always wish for their children to do and live better than themselves. You are like my son now; my adopted son. Perhaps, the story of my life will keep you from making the same mistakes that I made.

I hope you will learn a few things from the story of my life".

CHAPTER 4.

After listening to Uncle Tutu's story, Majid had several things going through his mind.

First, Uncle Tutu had disobeyed his mother's instructions by following bad company. That was a mistake and he paid dearly for it.

"We are told to honor, obey and respect our parents. Some day, when we become parents, we shall expect the same treatment from our own children," he reasoned.

Second, Uncle Tutu realized his mistakes and was willing to correct them and make amends. That was a step in the right direction.

"Everybody makes mistakes". There is a saying that *'it's not how many times a man falls that matters but how often and how well he is able to get back on his feet,'* he thought.

Third, there was a great need for cooperation between folks back home and those residing abroad. Without that cooperation, everybody would suffer one way or another. It is said that *'when the sky falls, it falls on everybody's head'.*

Then, he turned philosophical--
"Sometimes we act like the goat that values good habitat
Yet it amply soils its behind with ease.
We value good roads, good schools, and good hospitals
Yet, we pull down those ready to bring them to fruition;
We pretend that good things fall from the sky.
That's the irony of life!

We value good name, clean character, and unblemished record
Yet, we surround and fortify ourselves with endless deception and lies.
We pretend that truth can be buried forever
That's the irony of life!
We hate disappointments, rejection and failure
Yet, we'll kill shining candor and bring falsehood to life
In the process, we are turned into multiple vacuums filled with dancing shadows.
That's the irony of life!

For most of the day, Majid could not stop thinking about Uncle Tutu's life history.

He remembered his late mother, his childhood, and his fellow hawkers. He wondered how many of the hawkers might have been arrested, jailed, disabled, or even killed since he left the country. Or, if some of them might have found a better life.

He realized how *different* he was from Uncle Tutu. Even though both of them came from the same country, the two were as different in experience and objectives as day and night.

Uncle Tutu had a relatively normal childhood experience back home. Unlike Majid, he knew his father, and lived with a mother who was healthy all her life. He did not experience the brutality of street life; nor did he ever feel like a rat chased around the corner by bribe-seeking police constables. His parents did not die as a result of abject poverty and he never experienced the trauma and cruelty of being dumped and forgotten inside a prison. His soul was still *attached* to the homeland, and given the right conditions, Uncle Tutu would rather go back home than spend one extra day in America.

Majid, on the other hand, had experienced the worst aspects of life back home and had come to America to fight poverty to a logical end. He had *no* intention of going back to the same land that had denied him of all pride, dignity, and hope.

Majid was already in America and the time had come for him to fulfill his mission. However, one should not forget that America, like other countries in the world, had *poor* citizens as well as the rich. It was, therefore, unrealistic for some one to think that he or she could escape from poverty by simply getting to America.

'One does not catch a bird with bare hands,' the elders would say. To catch a bird, one would need some type of *an assault weapon*; a slingshot, a flying stick, a catapult, an arrow, a gun; something. In his quest to conquer poverty from the American soil, Majid was like someone trying to catch a bird and he needed some type of an *assault weapon*; the right connection, a high paying job, a generous inheritance, sheer luck, or exceptional knowledge and wisdom.

Obviously, he was not well-connected, was not a candidate for a high-paying job, and did not expect any lavish inheritance from family or close relatives.

He would have to depend on *luck* or some type of *exceptional knowledge and wisdom* to be able to fight and defeat poverty from the American soil. How good were his chances?

That night, Majid had an interesting dream. He was surrounded by a group of 'wise men', the same way his fellow hawkers surrounded him on the eve of his departure from home. The 'wise men', like his fellow hawkers, were there to 'celebrate' his recent success and also to 'advice' him on the most optimal ways to escape from poverty.

First, they partied all night eating; drinking and dancing. Then, they started to advice him, one after the other.

---*"To escape from poverty, you need to be financially self-sufficient and stable. To make that happen, you must not be afraid to fail. It's the adventurer, the inquisitive, and the optimistic person that keeps progressing while the apprehensive; the pessimistic quitter spends a lifetime trying to initiate a 'perfect' idea that might never take root. Don't be afraid to try something new,"* the first 'wise man' advised him.

---*"Waste is like fat which clogs up the recovery pipe. You must cut it off. There is a general tendency to waste everything big and small: water, food, time, energy, intelligence, air, resources, technology and all. Small wastes add up to one big, monstrous waste. Every item wasted is a loss for someone trying to escape from poverty. Don't be wasteful".*

That was from the second 'wise man'.

---*"Don't wait for success to come to you. Take the initiative.*

Success will circumvent and bypass the passive individual on its way to the aggressive. If you don't take the initiative, success might never come to you," said another, as others followed suit.

---*"Be a producer, not a consumer. To do that, you must-*

a. *Endeavor to be self-dependent. Do things for yourself and not wait for someone else to do them for you.*

b. *Avoid borrowing from others (except in extreme situations). And, when you do, pay back as soon as possible. A debt owed is a yoke and servitude incurred.*

c. *Re-invest extra proceeds and make them grow. Otherwise, they will lie dormant. Every extra proceed invested is a new proceed developed.*

If you follow the rules, you'll stop being a wholesale consumer," another counseled.

---*"Don't be a blind follower. It's said that 'no hairstyle fits every head'. Sometimes, being different from others can yield big dividends. Don't always discard your gut feelings in a blind preference to common practice," said yet another.*

---*"Don't go beyond your limits. No one is invincible. If it's too big for you, don't try it. If it's not working, try something else. If it's too ugly, back off. A person who embraces a fruitless venture is like someone crossing the line from reality to fantasy," said another.*

---*"Learn by observing and listening to others. You can learn a lot from other people's successes and failures," another 'wise' man recommended.*

---*"Always make room for plan B. There's always an alternative way of doing things. If one avenue closes, look for another one that is open. In the words of the elders, 'the rabbit credits his survival to a secondary exit hole'.*

That was from another 'wise man'.

---*"Define a contract before executing it. What is expected of you? How much are you getting paid? Are there any time limitations or deadlines? What happens if something goes wrong? Are you at liberty to sub-contract a job to another person? Establish clear terms of contract prior to the initiation of any job".*

That was the last 'advice' from the 'wise men' of the dream on how to escape from poverty.

When he woke up from his sleep, Majid felt like someone who had been through an educational seminar. He was reminded of the party held in his honor by his fellow hawkers on the eve of his departure from home.

Some of those 'wise men' in his dream looked very *familiar* and Majid wondered if they *were* the *same* fellow hawkers back home who might have come to his dream to assist him in his desire to escape from poverty.

Even *if* he could succeed in acquiring *an assault weapon* to fight poverty, Majid had yet one other pressing problem to deal with. He needed to change his *immigration status* from that of a temporary visitor to a permanent resident or a citizen. Time was not on his side.

One of the 'wise men' in his dream had already told him to *'always make room for plan B'.* He didn't have the legal means to change his immigration status. There had to be a 'plan B'. *Marrying an American citizen* sounded like the 'plan B' he needed to permanently legalize his stay in America.

He had already saved enough money to *initiate* the process of marriage. Hopefully, Uncle Tutu would be willing to assist him with extra financial help.

That evening, he shared his thoughts with Uncle Tutu.

"Uncle Tutu, where can I find an American wife?" he asked.

"There are American women all over the place. What type of wife are you looking for? You want someone to breast-feed you? You don't even have a roof over your head or a stable means of livelihood and you are looking for a wife! Have you forgotten the proverb that cautions: 'a turtle with its limitations should not take his bath with hot water'? You are trying to walk when you can't even crawl!"

"I hear that one can become a citizen by marrying an American wife," Majid responded.

"You need money to marry someone here unless you are looking for a homeless person like yourself. Even then, you still need money to marry her"

"How much money are we talking about?"

"Find yourself a lawyer and ask him or her that question. I'm not a lawyer"

"Where can I find a lawyer?"

"They are everywhere. Look at the yellow pages".

The day after the discussion on finding an American wife, Majid came across an advertisement which encouraged people to play the lottery and dream big with a dollar.

"A dollar can turn you into an instant millionaire". That was the advertisement.

Majid remembered one of the 'wise men' in his dream telling him: *"Don't wait for success to come to you. Take the initiative".*

A dollar, after all, was not worth much. He could spend a dollar without feeling a pinch. So, he took the initiative and played the lottery.

He knew he wasn't going to win; so he went home and forgot all about it. When the winning numbers were announced the following day, he became the sole winner!

He went from disbelief to ecstasy to confusion to tears of joy. Suddenly, he had more money than he could spend in two lifetimes.

What else could stop him from finding an American wife? He went straight to a lawyer to arrange a business marriage for him. It didn't matter who the business wife was. He had already *escaped from poverty.* He had one more *escape* to make. If he could legalize his stay in America, he would have succeeded in *escaping, permanently,* from the land that had roasted him from birth.

With plenty of money to spend, Majid had little or no problem finding an American woman to lead him to the altar of immigration freedom.

CHAPTER 5.

The first time his business wife called him 'honey', Majid felt very uneasy and threatened.

"I hope she is not going to eat me alive," he said to himself. He knew that back home married people had a tendency, or perhaps a habit, to call each other pet names: 'my moon', 'my heart', 'beautiful mother', 'pretty woman', 'love', 'mine', 'precious', etc. But, to call someone an edible name such as 'honey', 'sugar' or 'lemon' was something new to him.

It sounded like a *'handshake that had gone beyond the elbow'.*

"Soon, she might start calling me foo-foo as well! This is so embarrassing!" he pondered.

He knew little or nothing about the woman he married. The lawyer had assured him that the woman was a 'professional wife' who married men and divorced them to make a living. At the end of the business marital process, they would go their separate ways with no strings attached.

For better or for worse, his business wife turned out to be a good-natured and loving woman. From all indications, she was determined to be the best friend, best 'wife' and best partner to Majid. It was *rare* to get into such an ideal marital arrangement.

Most of the time, a business spouse in America would practically imprison, tantalize, humiliate, torture, and in the end, even disappoint his or her 'married' partner.

His wife's name was Sita. She was a florist who loved her job greatly. Industrious and innovative, Sita had quickly progressed from an employee who ran errands and delivered flowers for others to an employer who owned several flower shops of her own. By the time she married Majid, she already had scores of loyal employees who were working for her.

The couple lived together in the same house which Majid had purchased after winning the lottery. In cases where immigration papers had been filed on behalf a partner, immigration authorities had been known to pay surprise visits to ascertain that *both* husband and wife lived in the *same* place. So, the lawyer had advised them to live together until the successful resolution of their case.

On a typical evening when both of them came back from work, Sita would prepare the evening meal. After dinner, the couple would sit together, side by side, and simply chat, discuss the day's events, and watch television.

At the early part of their marriage, Majid was emotionally *detached* from the business woman she married and was only interested in using her to obtain his American citizenship. As time went on, he developed a strong genuine love for her.

Contrary to conventional wisdom, he started telling her every little secret of his life. He ignored the fact Sita could potentially use such information against him some day. Didn't the elders warn that *'when a man knows my strength, he wrestles me without tying his wrapper'*?

One day, Majid followed his wife to a church bazaar. The church was trying to raise some money and the congregants had been asked to contribute marketable items for sale at the bazaar. There were so many items on sale from various non-perishable food items to unused new clothing materials to school supplies. Christmas was around the corner and Majid went to a corner where someone was selling plastic Christmas trees of different sizes. There, he was accosted by an inquisitive seven-year old boy who bombarded him with rather unusual questions.

"Hey, mister; are you from Africa?" the little boy asked.
"Yes; I'm from Africa"
"Hey, mister; what's your name?"
"My name is Majid"
"Can I call you Mr. M?"
"Why? Don't you like the sound of my name?"

"You know those African names; they are such tongue twisters. I'll rather call you Mr. M"

"O.K.; if that will make you happy"

"What was it like swimming across the seas and oceans to come to America, Mr. M?"

"No one swims across the seas and oceans to come here from Africa. I came by air like everyone else"

"Is it true that you Africans live in caves and on top of trees?"

"We live in houses like everybody else. Sometimes, we even live in better houses than what you have here"

"Did you see your brother on television yesterday?"

"Which brother?"

"There was this North African man on television with a thick accent. I could hardly understand a word of what he was saying. I think he even mentioned your name"

"Listen boy, Africa is a continent, not a hamlet where every person knows everybody else. I have never even been to North Africa all my life! Besides, I don't even have a brother"

"Is it true that you share your filthy neighborhoods with rats and roaches; dogs and goats? You probably came to buy a Christmas tree to make you feel at home. Obviously, you must miss the bushes and all the animals that surround you back home in Africa"

"There's a proverb that says: 'A little bird dancing by the roadside has the drummer within'. Someone must have been polluting your mind; little boy. Some day, when you grow up, I hope you'll be better informed"

"Don't you eat other human beings?"

"No; we don't eat human beings. It is only the demented people who can do something like that and you'll find such people all over the world including here in America"

"So, you mean you don't actually sleep with those nasty and dangerous animals that surround you?"

"As a matter of fact, we do. You can go home and tell your mentor that we do sleep with animals, snakes and scorpions"

"And they don't bite you?"

"Of course, not; that would be against the law"

"Which law?"

"We have a law that protects everyone; humans and animals alike"

"Do the animals obey such a law?"

"Everybody obeys the laws; humans and animals alike. We demarcate the land with a wide white line painted on the ground. And we proclaim: "animals on one side; humans on the other". Any one, animal or human, who crosses the line will be breaking the law; and will be punished.

"How do you make the animals obey such a law? Do you tie them down or put them in a cage"

"That will amount to abuse of individual freedom"

"How then do you make them obey such a law?"

"Trying to explain such a process to you or to your mentor will amount to asking a new-born baby to fix a broken computer. This issue is too complicated for you and your mentor".

With that, Majid walked away from the inquisitive seven-year old boy.

CHAPTER 6.

That night, after a very delicious dinner, Majid and his wife kissed each other good night and went to their matrimonial bed.

In the middle of the night, Majid noticed something different about his wife's snoring. It sounded fictitious; like some type of 'fabricated' sound coming from the wind-pipe. Initially, he felt like waking her up. Then, he changed his mind. There was no point disturbing the woman from her 'sleep'. Not long after that, Majid went into deep sleep and had an awful dream.

In that dream, someone went after him and was determined to *severe* his head with an ax. The person looked like a male one minute; then a female the next. As he struggled to escape from his attacker, Majid quickly jerked out of his dream with an abbreviated yell. He could not sleep again for the rest of the night.

He didn't want to disturb his wife's sleep, so he waited till the morning to tell her about the dream. When the rays of daylight sliced through the window blinds, Majid knew that it was time to get up and out of bed. He felt like one being readied for the gallows.

"Good morning Honey," Sita greeted Majid.

"Good morning, my dear. How was your sleep?" he replied.

"I slept well. How was yours?" she asked.

He told her about the dream.

"You must be dreaming about your homeland. People don't get killed here with an ax but with guns. Don't let it bother you," she tried to reassure him

"Something tells me to be very careful today. Something else tells me not to leave this house at all. The last time I had a bad dream like this; I woke up and heard that my mother had been taken to the hospital. She did not come out of that hospital alive".

"You sound very superstitious," Sita mocked him.

"Our people say that 'When a snake bites a child, he begins to dread the head of a lizard'. I am scared," he re-echoed.

That morning, Majid dressed up to go to work as usual. With all the money he won from the lottery, he still went to work every day. He didn't want to join the rank of the *sadists* back home that were corrupted by money.

Though he had vowed never to go back home, he was already making plans to *send* home enough money to cater for his fellow hawkers.

He stepped out of his house into the driveway where his gray Toyota minivan was parked. He brought out the car key from his pocket and was about to unlock the car when a stranger came out of nowhere and stood beside him.

Startled into sudden fright, Majid stood still; frozen, as he sucked in the air of desperation. The stranger pointed the muzzle of a handgun at him, hissed a warning sound for him to remain silent, and waved him into the driver's seat.

"Sssh," the man hushed him

"Open the car and get inside. If you value your life, don't act funny or smart," he ordered Majid.

It was a tall hooded man wearing a dark mask. Careful not to provoke the stranger into pulling the trigger or doing something lethal, Majid quietly unlocked his car and sat behind the steering wheel. Simultaneously, the hooded stranger followed suit and entered the back of the car with the handgun pointing menacingly at Majid.

From the corner of his eye, Majid could see his wife, Sita, watching the entire incident from their second floor bedroom window. That gave him some *relief.* Help would soon be on the way.

"Follow my instructions. Start the car, and drive," the armed man ordered him.

Majid complied with the order.

As soon as Majid backed out of the driveway, he noticed another car with tinted windows parked near his driveway. As he drove away from his house on instructions, he noticed the second car following closely behind him.

No one in the neighborhood suspected anything. He passed several cars on the road and wished he could alert someone of his precarious situation. But, he couldn't. There was a gun pointed at him.

The only person he could depend upon to sound an alarm was his wife. She had witnessed everything that went on. She must have called the police. If she failed to call the police, he would be entirely on his own.

When they got to a wooded area, the armed hooded man ordered Majid to slow down and drive the car into a dark alley. When they got to the darkest zone, Majid was ordered to stop the car and pull over by the side.

Meanwhile, the second car was still trailing them.

"When was the last time you said your prayers?" the hooded stranger asked

"This morning when I got out of bed," Majid replied.

"Do you do that every morning when you wake up?"

"I do that every night before I sleep and every morning when I wake up"

"What do you pray for?"

"First, I always thank God for His numerous blessings to me. I thank God for yesterday, today and tomorrow. At night, I ask God to take care of my soul if I die in my sleep. In the morning, I thank Him for letting me see another day. And finally, I always pray for my wife's wellbeing," Majid responded.

"If I ask you to say your last prayers right now, what will be your prayer?" the hooded stranger asked.

"I will first thank God for his numerous favors to me. Then I will pray that His will be done".

"You are a good Christian, aren't you?"

"Only God can answer that question. I simply try my best to be a good, decent human being".

"Because you seem to be a good decent human being, I'm going to do you one big favor. I want you to say your last prayers; silently. You don't have to tell me what those prayers are and I will give you enough time to make peace with your God".

"Why should I be saying my last prayers?" Majid asked; his quivering voice reduced to whispers.

"Because you are going to die," the stranger replied.

"But, why? To the best of my knowledge, I don't think I have offended anybody".

"You are not in a court of law. Close your eyes and say your last prayers".

There was silence between the two.

A few minutes later, the stranger cocked the gun and ordered Majid to start the car and drive deeper into the bush. He complied with the order. The second car followed suit.

A few yards into the bush, the stranger ordered Majid to stop the car and come out with his hands clasped behind his head. As soon as he stepped out of his car, the driver of the second vehicle approached him with a rope in his hand.

"Lie down with your face on the ground," the armed man ordered him.

As soon as his body touched the ground, the man with the rope tied his hands behind the back.

The gun was fired.

Quickly, Majid felt wet soil sprinkled over his body; and passed out.

When he regained consciousness, he saw himself lying in a hospital bed. Standing beside him were two constables in police uniform.

Dazed, surprised and partly disoriented, he looked around trying to figure out where he was. He fixed his gaze on one of the constables. Then, with a hesitant finger pointing at the constable, he muttered a few words:

"Please tell me I'm dead".

"You are dead. In fact, you are not only dead. Your corpse has already been deposited in the hospital mortuary waiting to be

identified and claimed by your family," the constable replied with a cold face.

Majid looked at himself from all angles. He touched and squeezed the different parts of his body trying to ascertain their viability or lack of it.

"Am I really dead?" he asked the constable with a resigned look on his face.

"Let me introduce myself to you. I am inspector Sand and here with me is sergeant Tibi. We are from the criminal division of the police department. You must be surprised to see us standing beside you in a hospital room".

"Surprise is not the right word, inspector. Try confusion, disorientation, or hallucination. I feel like a schizophrenic. Am I really dead; or alive? Please someone tell me what is going on"

"As you can see, you are very much alive and well.

Between you, the hospital and the police department, we all know that you are alive and well. However, the rest of the world out there is hearing something different. The news hitting the air waves right now is that someone who fits your description died in a wooded area near your home with bullet wounds to the head; and that the person's gray Toyota minivan was found at the crime scene. Your name has not been released, and will not be released. This way, the general public does not know who you are or even where you live. The hospital staff does not know your true identity either; at least not yet. All they know is that you are a patient admitted to the hospital for exhaustion and observation. Right now, you don't have to do anything except eat, sleep and relax. We will handle the rest".

"I'm confused, officer," he managed to say.

"That's understandable," the officer replied.

"How did you get involved with this matter in the first place?" Majid asked.

"Someone called us to your rescue; someone who cares about you," the officer replied.

"Someone who cares about me?"

"Yes; someone who cares about you"

"I knew my wife would come to my rescue! She saw everything from our second floor bedroom window; how I was kidnapped at

gun point by a masked man. I'm blessed with a most wonderful wife, officer. She calls me 'honey'. We've never argued except to protect each other's interest. What could I ever do without her? Is there any way I can call her and ask her to come and get me, officer?" he asked.

"You can't call anybody yet," the officer replied.

"Why not, officer?" he asked.

"All of your questions will be answered in due course. For now, remain calm, relax, eat, rest and leave the rest to us".

"How can I relax; eat and rest in a hospital room when my wife doesn't even know where I am. I can imagine how worried she is right now".

"We shall get to her on your behalf; if that will make you feel better"

"Thank you, officer. That is kind of you"

"You need to thank someone else, not me".

With that, both officers walked out of the room leaving a grateful Majid wondering what was happening to him.

"Someone called us to your rescue; someone who cares about you". Those words kept ringing in his ears. He couldn't stop wondering what was going on--

"Am I a victim of mistaken identity? Is someone framing me up for something I didn't do? How safe is my wife; alone, in that house when I'm being held prisoner in a hospital room? Why will someone declare him dead while I'm still alive and well? How safe am I in this hospital room?"

Majid had never been so confused and bewildered in his entire life.

CHAPTER 7.

Back in the house, Sita turned on the television and flipped through the different channels. They all had the same 'newsflash'.

A man that fitted her husband's description was found, shot in the head, in a wooded area of the central community. The victim's gray Toyota minivan was found at the crime scene. The victim's identity was not released and his body had already been deposited in an unnamed hospital mortuary. Apparently, he must have been killed by armed robbers.

Sita was in the living room with her eyes glued to the television, and she was all alone when the door bell rang twice; then once.

She waited.

Again, the door bell rang twice; then once.

That sounded like a coded password from the visitor.

She went to the door, turned the knob, and quickly let the visitor into the living room.

"Good day Madam," the stranger greeted her.

"Good day to you, too," she replied.

"You have a package for me, Madam?"

"Sure. I do; with gratitude. There's a little extra something in there for you," she responded.

A small package exchanged hands quickly. It was all business, with little ceremony; no handshakes, and no smiles, no hugs or kisses.

Within minutes, the man was gone from the house.

If Sita had any emotions, she took great pains to suppress them.

She was the one who always told her husband to be 'suspicious' of the walls, and the surroundings.

"You never know which walls or surroundings might have eyes, or ears," she had always cautioned Majid.

She sat down, expectantly, in a leather couch. If she was waiting for something to happen, she chose to be patient.

Half an hour later, the door bell rang. This time, it rang only once. That was the common, traditional way of ringing people's door bells.

She turned off the television before going to the door. When she opened the door, she saw two police constables; a male and a female.

"Good day madam," the female constable greeted her.

"Good day officers, can I help you?" she replied calmly, with a suspicious look on her face.

"Does Majid live here by any means?" the officer asked.

"Yes. Majid is my husband. Is there any problem?"

"Can we come in?"

"Most certainly! Is there any problem? We have never been visited by police officers before. Is my husband alright? What happened to him?" she followed one question with another.

The officers followed Sita to the living room and asked her to sit down

"Please tell me officers; is there any problem?" she persisted, with a face of increasing anxiety.

"There is a little problem," the male officer replied.

"I knew it! We've never had a police officer come to this house. Is he involved in an accident?"

"He had a little accident. Luckily, he had his identity card and address in his pocket. With that, we were able to trace his house"

"What happened to him, officer?" she asked frantically.

"Calm down, Madam. You need to follow us to the location where he is"

"Where is he, officer?" she asked hysterically pulling the male constable by the uniform.

"First calm down, get yourself together, and we will tell you everything".

"OK, I will calm down," she said slowing down the breathing.

"Sit down, Madam, please," the male officer pleaded.

She sat down.

"Your husband is dead. You need to come with us to the mortuary and identify his remains".

There was silence followed by a sudden terrifying expression on her face. One would think she was suddenly possessed by the devil.

"My husband is dead and I need to follow you to the mortuary and identify his remains?"

"Yes Madam. Please calm down," the female officer pleaded.

"How can you ask me to calm down? Isn't it said that 'whatever affects the nose brings tears to the eyes'? My husband is dead and you're asking me to calm down?"

"Madam; please calm down"

"It's easy for you to say. You're not the one that lost a spouse. It is said that 'when the corpse of another person's child is lifted, it looks like a piece of log'.

"Madam, we understand what you're going through"

"No, you don't. You're not the one in grief. 'A child strapped on the back of the mother does not know how difficult it is to walk'. Who killed him; you?"

"No Madam. We didn't kill him. He was shot by an unknown assassin. I know how difficult this must be for you. But, you need to come with us to the mortuary".

Suddenly, Sita flared up like a maniac. She was all over the floor, rolling herself from one end to the other. Then, she stood up and threw herself on the couch. Her pains and anguish were palpably hard to contain. The officers took great pains to keep her from sustaining any physical injury.

After several minutes of intense physical battle, the drama died down and Sita followed them to the hospital.

CHAPTER 8.

On their way to the hospital, the male officer stopped temporarily to speak to Sita.

"Be strong, madam. I know this is very difficult for you. It's going to get even more difficult as time goes on. Life is full of surprises. Sometimes, we smile and jubilate as things work in our favor. Other times, we become helpless losers in a world of chess and uncertainties. Be strong, madam"

"Is this the way to the mortuary, officer?"

"Yes," he replied.

Sita had never been to a mortuary before and had no idea what it looked like.

She had heard people describe the mortuary in different terms; a cold room with dead bodies stacked up, frozen, one on top of each other; a large walk-in freezer with individual remains laid out on stretchers waiting to be collected; a large room filled with dead bodies in separate body bags.

Traditionally, people *dreaded* the thought of going to the mortuary or even coming in contact with a dead body.

In her mind, a mortuary should be completely *isolated*, distant and hidden from the main hospital and from public view.

Back at the hospital where Majid was staying, the two police constables re-entered his room. This time, they came with a fierce-looking, thick-muscled stranger who looked like a hardened criminal.

"*We brought along someone who might be helpful,*" one of the officers said to Majid as soon as they re-entered the room.

"*What is going on? What is happening to me?*" he asked.

"*Relax and don't panic. All of your questions will be answered in due course*"

"*Can I please call my wife?*" he requested once again.

"You'll be speaking to her shortly"

"Thanks, officer".

Meanwhile, Sita and the two Police constables had arrived at the hospital and were minutes away from Majid's hospital room.

"*This is the room where you will come face-to-face with your husband,*" the male officer informed Sita.

"*Officer, must I enter this room with you?*" she asked, resisting the officer's attempt to take her along.

"*What choice do you have, Madam? You are here to positively identify your husband. Get yourself together*".

When they got to the door of the hospital room where Majid was staying, the male officer tapped gently on the door.

"*Come in, please,*" someone responded.

The door was flipped open.

Sita's face was covered with fresh tears; her face furrowed with multiple frowns and sad looks. She was expecting to see her husband's corpse wrapped in a body bag inside a hospital mortuary. She looked haggard and disheveled with rumpled outfit and dirty hair.

Quickly, she came face to face with her husband who was very much alive in the midst of two police constables and a stranger. Her husband was sitting on the hospital bed and appeared like someone in a trance. Sita's reaction was as spontaneous as it was informative and transparent.

She quickly lost her color and coordination; her speech became slurred. With great effort and difficulty, she pointed a reluctant finger first at her husband and then at the stranger.

"*My God! You're alive!*" she shouted at her husband with great shock.

"*Thank God you're here!*" the husband responded with an obvious relief.

"And you! What are you doing here?" she bellowed at the stranger, her face filled with hate.

"Don't tell me you double-crossed me. How could you do this to--"

She couldn't finish her sentence.

Her legs gave way as she folded like a soft banana leaf and collapsed on the floor. The police officers caught her in time and laid her down on her husband's hospital bed.

The nurse, who was quickly notified, took her vital signs and called the Doctor.

Meanwhile, Sita slipped in and out of consciousness. She would temporarily open her eyes; look at her surrounding, and pass out once again.

The Doctor arrived and asked everybody but her husband to leave the room for a few minutes while he examined her. She had shallow breathing with elevated pulse and systolic blood pressure. The Doctor placed an oxygen mask on her face and instructed the nurse to bring the emergency cart. Quickly, the Nurse complied with the order. As soon as the Doctor started the intravenous fluid, he added some medication to it to stabilize the visitor-turned-patient.

"It's alright. Don't panic. I'm the Doctor," he said quickly to Sita as she reluctantly opened her eyes.

"You are in a state of extreme shock. I have given you some medication to calm your nerves, stabilize your vital signs, and stop you from slipping in and out of consciousness. You are going to be alright," the Doctor reassured her.

"Doctor, am I dreaming? Is this for real?" she managed to ask.

She was a lot calmer and relaxed. The medication must have suppressed the intense feelings of shock, anger, disappointment and desperation.

"All you need to do right now is relax. You can withhold your questions for now," the Doctor replied.

"Can your visitors come back in?" the Doctor asked her pointing at the door.

"Ask him. They are his visitors, not mine," she answered pointing at her bewildered husband.

The Doctor was equally confused.

"Can they come in now, sir?"

"Frankly, I don't know what to say," Majid replied.

"Oh let them come in! The past is gone; the future must be confronted," Sita stepped in.

The police constables and the stranger were allowed in once again.

"I should have known that I was dealing with a criminal and a betrayer; someone who will receive payment even for double-crossing you. What a shameless man!" Sita said angrily.

"Those who perpetuate evil and thrive in the destruction of human lives should be ready to stand the heat when things work against them," the stranger fired back.

"Go ahead and mock me now that I've suddenly become your victim," she replied; this time speaking directly to the stranger.

"This naive gentleman, who has no idea what is going on right now, saved my life once and I embraced the first opportunity to return the favor. He deserves a full explanation of what has been going on in his life.

The time has come for him to know the truth; and that time is now," the stranger said directly to Sita while pointing at her husband.

In the ensuing silence, the room suddenly felt like a graveyard.

Minutes later, the stranger continued from where he stopped. This time, he spoke directly to Majid.

"I will start by introducing myself. My name is Babs. I am a professional hit man. I am trained to maim, dismember or eliminate real, potential and imagined adversaries or enemies. That is what I do for a living. Because I am so good at what I do, I don't demand payment until a job is completed.

In my type of job, because I don't mix business with pleasure, I don't get romantically involved with my female clients.

I met you under the strangest of circumstances. There was this group of cultists that had double-crossed my gang and waylaid a bounty that was meant for us. We gave them an ultimatum--to give up our bounty or prepare for a bloody war. That was when they sent their representative to discuss an amicable settlement with us.

As the head of my gang, I had come to meet with their representative to resolve the potentially explosive situation. During that meeting, the criminal who was sent to meet with me suddenly pulled a gun on me. At that very moment, a total stranger, came out of nowhere and placed himself between me and the armed man, pleading for my life. That stranger happened to be you. I'm sure you remember that incident very well. The moment you stepped in-between us the armed criminal backed down and walked away from the scene without firing a single bullet. He was as stunned as I was by your behavior.

I was baffled. Several questions went through my mind. Who was this stranger? Who or what sent him to save my life? What made the armed criminal back down in the first place? Why would a stranger risk his life for someone he did not know? You vanished from the scene just as fast as you had appeared without giving me a chance to know who you were, or to even thank you for saving my precious life.

Sita here has been my client for so many years. A proverb says that 'whoever stays closest to you will perceive the odor of your mouth the most'. No one, not even you as her present husband, can claim to know this woman better than myself. No one should be deceived by her gentle demeanor. It is said that 'the fingers of a hand can be gentle and harmless until they are turned into a fist'. As harmless as she may look, this woman can be vicious. It is true that 'those who climb with their teeth know the taste of bitter trees'. This woman is a criminal and she understands violence. For years, I singularly advanced her business of maiming and kidnapping people for ransom. I personally forced his business associates, opponents and competitors into letting her reign supreme in the floral industry.

At a point in time, my criminal activities caught up with me and I paid a hefty price by going to jail. While in jail, I was reformed from a hardened criminal to a child of God. I renounced my evil ways and I tried to reform Sita as well. Her response was flatly negative. She said I had been 'brainwashed' behind bars and that I could never 'subdue' her mind the same way. I was her ace card in *the world of crimes and she was not going to lose my services without a fight. So, she fought back ferociously. Sita engaged the services of a hypnotist and a juju priest to 'free' my mind and enforce my continued loyalty to her.*

Unfortunately for her, my transformation was too deep-rooted to be reversed by hypnotism, sorcery or intimidation.

Sita kept throwing her 'jobs' at me and I kept refusing them. One day, she begged me to do her one last favor.

"Carry out this one last assignment for me and I will never bother you again," she promised.

Though she is a criminal, Sita is a woman who never breaks her promise.

She wanted me to eliminate her husband; a man I did not know. Her husband, she said, had just won this lottery that was worth millions of dollars. She wanted him dead so she could collect all the money.

"This is the last time I will ever ask you to do something like this. This job is so important to me that it must get done. I want you to do it because you are the best in the business. Your reward this time around will be more than handsome and with it, both of us can quit the crime business once and for all. Since you have turned into a religious fanatic, I will absolve you of all criminal responsibilities and invoke God's anger and wrath on myself. Hopefully, this will make the job a little easier for you," she said to me.

She had a hard time convincing me to take this 'last' job. Eventually, I agreed to do it; if only to silence her criminal behavior.

Then, she gave me your picture and I recognized you instantly.

That was when the tables turned against her and I decided to do the right thing.

First, I had to stop her from getting you killed. At the same time, I didn't want to see anybody harmed; not even Sita herself.

Secondly, I saw this as an opportunity to repay your incredible favor to me. You saved my life. It was time for me to save yours as well.

Thirdly, I had to protect myself from Sita. If she had any suspicion of my motives, she would hire an alternative hit man, get rid of me and still accomplish her objective. I told Sita I would do the job for her. At the same time, I notified the police and they agreed to work with me.

To carry out the purported murder, I was wearing a mask and a hood when I accosted you in your driveway as you were about to enter your car. My accomplice was a police constable sitting in a tinted vehicle that was parked near the driveway. I could see Sita watching the whole episode from a second floor window of the house. She must have been convinced beyond any reasonable doubt that nothing could go wrong.

The news of her husband's "death" on television strengthened her conviction that the job had been perfectly carried out. She was so elated at the news that when I sent my agent to collect payment for the job, she happily gave him twice the amount that had been agreed upon. She thought she was going to acquire millions of dollars after killing you. Unfortunately for her, she ignored a proverb that says: 'the illness that kills someone will follow the person to the grave'. She could not destroy you without destroying her herself as well.

When the police visited her in the house, a visit she had anticipated, she must have acted like a distraught widow whose husband meant everything to her. She was eager to identify his dead body and collect the booty. One can only imagine the shock she felt when she came face to face with a husband who was completely healthy, alive and well. Her shock must have been magnified several fold by the sight of me sitting side by side with you; the intended victim.

There's a proverb that says: 'If an individual cooks for the community, the community will finish the food. But, if a community cooks for an individual, he or she cannot finish it'. Right now, your beloved wife is fighting alone against a community; a war she cannot win. I am hopeful that she, too, will receive God's forgiveness and be reformed in jail like I was. If that happens, ours will be an awful story that ended well for everybody. I believe that every nagging question has been adequately answered. I will now let the police constables perform their duties. Thank you".

Silence--

"Take her away in handcuffs. She is going to spend the rest of her life in jail," the most senior constable eventually broke the silence.

"Wait officer; I need some answers from her. Tell me why you wanted to kill me because of money," Majid asked his business wife.

"You will never understand," she replied.

"Try me," he insisted with a stern face.

"I don't have anything in common with you. You once quoted your elders as saying that 'a twig which embraces a palm tree should know that they could never be siblings'. I was never interested in you. I had only one mission: to find an escape from poverty! All my life, I have borne the crushing weight of poverty. The home where I grew up could be described as a war zone. I was raised in the midst of drugs, sex, violence, alcoholism, police brutality, guns and gunfire. I lived with rats, mice and cockroaches. I ate out of dustbins and garbage dumps. While children my age went to school and shared the love of a happy family, I roamed around the streets counting the days I stayed alive. Being a florist was a mere smokescreen for my illegal activities. It is a mystery that I could live long enough to recount my ordeal.

Unfortunately, you didn't know the lady you were married to. I never had a decent education. I spend a greater part of my life contracting business marriages hoping to catch a rich man in the process. I could never find a decent job for someone my age. Every job demands experience, education or training; something that I don't have. Why do you think I don't have a permanent home of my own with my own husband and children? You think I care whether I go to jail or not? I have spent my entire life jailed by destitution, poverty and despair. Which jail could be worse than that? I have been jailed by violence. I have been jailed by hopelessness. I have been jailed by the extreme horrors of life. Frankly speaking, I didn't enjoy hurting an honest and simple man like you. Rather, I was desperately trying to escape from poverty. And, when the opportunity came, I grabbed it; the same way a drowning person would cling to a straw in the middle of a violent sea. Officer, please take me away from here"

"Not so fast! You thought I would never understand, right? Well, you are wrong!

You were trying to escape from poverty; so was I.

Why would a man like me forsake everything dear to him, risk everything including his own life, and travel thousands of miles to come to America with little or no hope of ever living a normal life?

You were trying to *escape from poverty*; so was I.

Why would a man pick a strange woman from the street and take her home as a wife just to change his immigration status?

I have slept with poverty. I have felt it. I've sniffed it. I have touched it, and tasted it. I have been pushed, bitten, shoved, slapped, kicked, and battered by poverty. I have tried and failed to negotiate my way out of poverty. I have tried and failed to get reprieve from poverty. I have tried and failed to regain freedom from the shackles of poverty. I lived a life much worse than that of a dog that I once walked and gave bath every morning. That dog became my master, my employer, and my source of livelihood. I have been jailed for being at the wrong place at the wrong time. I was once rejected by a mother who could no longer afford to take care of me. Only a spontaneous smile from my face could change her mind. My mother told me so. When I was barely a teenager, my mother died on a cold hospital floor. She was refused treatment for lack of funds. My father borrowed the money he used to marry my mother and ultimately died in jail for failing to repay that loan on time. I know what it means to be deprived of the very basic necessities of life. Who, in your shoes or mine, would reject any opportunity to escape from poverty?"

"Can we take her away now?" the officer asked.

"No, officer; don't take her away. I will not press any charges against her. I will give her a second chance to come clean".

Majid then addressed Sita once again.

"It is said that 'when the eagle begins to eat corpses, toad and millipedes, it can no longer distinguish itself from the vulture'. I didn't come to America to put someone in jail. Such an act should be reserved for the heartless and the sadistic. Now that we have plenty of money, none of us should go to jail or die because of it. You can have half of it, walk out of my life, and live happily ever after. You have no further excuse or reason after today to hurt, maim, or kill another person for the rest of your life. You remind me of the saying that 'if a poor man is allowed into

a garden-egg farm, he plucks everything at once'. The smell of a million dollars turned you into an insatiable monster.

Your loyal hit-man had to experience life in jail in order to change from bad to good. You don't need to go to jail to undergo the same transformation. I would have preferred to keep you, love you, and cherish you as a wife; especially now that we have discovered each other straight from the pit of hell. However, a union between husband and wife should be voluntary; not obligatory".

At this juncture, Sita fell on her knees before Majid.

"I never knew I could ever kneel before a fellow human being to ask for forgiveness. I had the means and the temperament to subjugate others at will. I was heartless, brutal, insensitive and indifferent. However, there's one thing in my sordid life that I'll always be proud of-- I've never said anything I didn't mean. I have never broken a single promise. I am sorry; truly sorry for what I have done; and I mean every word of it. Though I don't deserve to be your real wife, if you ever decide to take me back, I will promise to be the best possible wife I could ever be to a man. If, on the other hand, you'd rather live your life without me, I'll walk out of your life and never hurt another human being for the rest of my life. And, that's a promise! I don't deserve half of your money; not after what I have done. You can keep all of it. You have already given me something much bigger and better than money. You have jailed my ugly past. In the process, you have transformed my life for the better".

Majid helped her to her feet.

"Please get up. I think I may have found me a true wife. It is said that 'the tooth occasionally bites the tongue. Yet, they must co-exist within the same mouth'. Sometimes, we find salvation where we least expect it. Sometimes, that which we value the least will turn out to be the corner stone of our life.

I will take you home and make things work between us. I will love you, and cherish you; and together we will bring forth children in an atmosphere of love and happiness. From the embers of poverty and degradation, we have both sprouted into a vibrant new life. We have captured, dismembered and buried our common enemy-- poverty.

Our gratitude goes to you, the hit-man-turned-angel-of-mercy who stepped in to save my life and paved the way for this mutual discovery and reconciliation. You, too, will benefit from our good luck.

Our gratitude goes to you, the police officers who collaborated with a stranger in a tight-lipped operation to carry out your assignment to a logical conclusion.

Come, my wife; and take my hand. This hand now belongs to you. Our people say that, 'when something bigger than yam is found, the barn is sold off'. I have found something bigger and better than money. I have found you. Better still, we have both found each other. And, we have both escaped from poverty. Together, we shall turn around and put poverty to shame, degrade it and put it away; forever".

Sita responded with great emotions.

"You once quoted a proverb saying that 'the right hand washes the left while the left washes the right'. You have 'washed' me completely.

First, you bleached off my stains of violence and deception. Then, you granted me an unconditional and undeserved amnesty. As if that was not enough, you opened your arms wide to share your life with me and accept me the way I am. And, this was after I had paid someone to kill you.

You have washed me clean. Now, out of reverence for the elders in their wisdom, it is my turn to wash you clean as well. I want to serve as a catalyst toward a final and lasting reconciliation between you and your roots.

Promise me that some day when the time is right for you, we shall re-locate to the land of your birth.

Our children, even if they remain behind, deserve to know their roots.

Your people back home, even if they have offended you, deserve a relationship with you.

Your late parents, even though they are deceased, will find comfort in their graves knowing that their beloved son did not get lost in a foreign land.

Make me that promise and you will make me the happiest wife in the whole world"

Majid responded in kind.

"Some day, I will take home the most wonderful wife I found in America. That is my promise. Together, we will find peace and *comfort in the same land of wisdom where the elders stood the test of time. You have, indeed, reformed and washed me completely. The elders were right when they said that 'the right hand washes the left while the left washes the right'.*

About the Author

Charles Onyegbule Uzoaru,M.D. is a graduate of Columbia University, New York (1974), and the University of Pennsylvania School of Medicine, Philadelphia (1977). He is a practicing Obstetrician/Gynecologist. His first novel, "Behind a Timid Mask", was published in 2005. His book, "Road to a Happy Marriage", was published in 2011.

ABOUT THE BOOK

Majid was born and brought up in Africa, a continent where the super-rich brazenly rubbed wealth on the faces of the poor while the downtrodden suffered immensely. Out of frustration and in his quest to travel to America, Majid gave up everything that was dear to him. America, he was told, was a land where streets were paved with gold and money grew on trees. It didn't matter to him if he ended up maimed, jailed, disabled or killed in the process of getting to the land of milk and honey. What else was he living for?

"Born in Africa" is an expose of life in Africa, the wide gap between the rich and the poor, and the tales of a new African immigrant in America.